THROUGH A HEDGE BACKWARDS

"More Glory to God"

by

John Jacklin

British Library Cataloguing in Publication Data.
A catalogue record for this book is available from the British Library

ISBN 978 0 86071 693 8

A Commissioned Publication of

tel: 0115 932 0643 web: www.moorleys.co.uk

Acknowledgements

I would like to give my special thanks to Moorleys, Bob Lunt, Michael and Pauline Huggins, and members of the Parish who have helped me, including Ray Tew for his photos. Plus of course my wife Ann, for her tremendous and unfailing support over the years. I wish to dedicate this book to all clergy, and all those congregations who struggle to make the Church relevant to their communities in this country today.

"Where things impossible by God shall be made possible,
so let's give the glory unto to Him!"
(Variation on words by Graham Kendrick)

CONTENTS

PREFACE

My main reason for writing this second book is to relate what God continues to do as I have sought to be in the place of His choice. Also to show that this does not obviate the problems that will come our way even as we choose to take the path He sets out for us. Our enemy the Evil One, will always devise all sorts of ways to dishearten us and frequently place obstacles in our way. I also know from my own experience that the Church overseas has so much to teach and encourage us.

On returning to the U.K. after serving the Lord in South America for 13 years I found the Anglican Church here so different - or rather so behind - the Church in Chile.

In England we are hindered by many problems. Some are due to congregations, some by communities, some by clergy, and some by dioceses. Once a Churchwarden apparently said "We've had so many changes here over the past thirty years and I have opposed every one of them!" Yet, in my experience, it was so refreshing to find one bishop who said to me "John don't ask me if you can do it, just tell me afterwards."

One great set back is that the Church of England here carries so much baggage. Our cathedrals and ancient Churches are a great heritage and include many beautiful buildings. But these are a constant drain on our income and resources and are also subject to so many regulations. The Anglican Church in Chile has the advantage that it does not have lots of large or expensive cathedrals, ancient palaces or buildings.

Last year at the induction of a Chilean Clergyman in Ipswich his Rector said in my hearing "I'm afraid my new colleague will find it difficult to cope with all the faculties here." To which one elderly English cleric responded "Oh I wouldn't worry too much, I've been losing my faculties for years!"

Two of the biggest pastoral challenges I encountered in England were baptisms and burials. I mean what biblical basis can there be for baptising an infant where the parents are not even Christians? Burials in a large Churchyard are also a nightmare when one tries to cope with the regulations and maintenance. Why doesn't the government take responsibility for Churchyards? After all, a Churchyard is really a local cemetery. The clergy will then be able to do get on with the task they were called and trained for, namely preaching the Gospel and giving pastoral care to the people in their Parishes. Yet in the midst of much frustration I saw people coming to a personal relationship with Jesus. Especially the 16 people converted at the Billy Graham Campaign in Sheffield, and others brought to Christ through a student mission from Ridley Hall, Cambridge.

FOREWORD

John Jacklin had just returned from Chile when we first met. We were Curates in neighbouring Parishes and I was excited to meet him and Ann because my wife and I were thinking of applying to the South American Mission Society (SAMS) to serve in South America. The story of his time in Chile is told in his book *"Gloria a Dios"*, which is a refreshingly honest account of missionary work.

This book continues in the same vein as John recounts his experiences back in England as a new curate and then as an incumbent. His style is conversational, as if he was sitting in his living room and he is telling stories about his ministry and reflecting on what he has learnt. Sometimes, of course, there is no real learning except that people can be strange and difficult. But that is the joy of this book.

Many of us, whether we are in full time parochial ministry or not, will find resonances from our own lives. Hopefully it will prompt us to be honest and open about our feelings and bring them to God. John has a way of drawing us into his life which makes us want to go on reading. This is not a deeply theological book, but certainly it deals with theological and pastoral issues and real human relationships.

Above all, the theme is the same as John's first book; even though at times his ministry felt like being dragged through a hedge backwards, there is still the overall confidence in a good God who leads and provides for His people. We can still say at the end of this book: *"Gloria a Dios"!*

Bishop Henry Scriven
South American Director for the Church Mission Society (incorporating SAMS)

Chapter 1
CHRIST CHURCH, HARROW

My parents
William & Florence Jacklin

Job Search

Coming to the end of our time in Chile I had to give some serious thought to what I would do back in England. The option that most attracted me was to work as a full time hospital Chaplain. But if this was not possible then I would work at my old secular job during the day and be a N.S.M. (Non Stipendiary Minister) in the evenings and weekends. I had no desire to get involved in the parochial system of the Church of England. So I wrote to a lady I had previously known in Blackheath who was secretary to a body that appointed hospital chaplains. She replied that full time chaplaincies were few and far between. Most chaplains were part time and on the staff of a Parish, or worked at a secular job in the daytime. So that was the end of my being a full time Hospital Chaplain.

On the way home from Chile we had decided to call to see Anthony and Alison Smyth with whom we had worked in the Anglican Centre in Chile. Anthony was then working in Peru so when the ship docked at Callao we got a taxi from the port to their home in Lima. During conversation Anthony showed me a letter he had received from the Rev Eddie Shirras concerning a curacy at Christ Church, Harrow. "I'm not interested" Anthony said. "But if you are why not go for it?" Later I also received a letter through the post from Eddie. I discovered he was a friend of Canon

Philip King, the then General Secretary of the South American Missionary Society.

Eddie had presumably asked if there were any missionaries coming back to England who would be looking for a job. I must confess that in my subconscious mind I still felt the Lord had called me to be a missionary, and this had not changed whatever the future held for me. Before this, to my surprise, I was offered a curacy in Slough but I decided to go for an interview with Eddie. He had until recently been Assistant General of the Church Pastoral Aid Society and had just been appointed Vicar of Christ Church, Roxeth in South Harrow. I went for two interviews and following the second Eddie invited me to join him.

Interview with the Bishop

After the interviews with Eddie I had to see the Bishop of Willesden. He was genuinely interested in us as a family and asked lots of questions about the work we had been doing in South America. The interview lasted almost three hours during which he made copious notes on a clip board. He said finally "Are there any questions you would like to ask?" Here was my opportunity. For I had been thinking for some time I would like to do some further theological training, so I broached the subject. In fact I had discovered that Christ Church, Roxeth had two Harrow masters in the congregation, plus several professional actors, which all made me feel a little inferior to the task. Hewlett Thompson had listened attentively to my question and then asked "Who do you think might pay for that?" I replied I had no idea and began to think that what I wanted was not going to happen. But all was not lost because he went on to say "Well I will make further training a condition of you coming into my diocese and we shall pay for it." He then explained that there was money set aside from the sale of a college in Cheshunt that could only be used for theological training. I was thrilled to bits and could see the Lord's hand was providing for me. However, reporting back to Eddie I could see he wasn't too pleased at my having Tuesday and one weekend a month at Oak Hill, plus a day off as well.

The Curate's House

The Curate's house was at that time occupied by the Rev Andrew Kirk and family, missionaries recently home from Argentina. So for the first few weeks back in England we stayed with my parents in Blackheath. Once the house became vacant we stayed with Ann's dad in St Albans, commuting each day to get on with redecorating the house. Ann's Dad was very supportive and accompanied us each day to get the job done as quickly as possible. One day Peter and I were working upstairs as Ann's Dad had decided that we should line the back bedroom ceiling. Dad got on with the paintwork downstairs because his arthritis made it difficult for him to climb ladders. Peter and I worked all of one morning struggling to get our first piece of lining paper to stick to the ceiling. Our problem was as fast as we got one end up, and turned round, we found it had come down and was hanging round our necks! After several hours we were absolutely fed up - then Dad called up the stairs "Come down you two, the sausage and bacon is getting cold." Eventually he got fed up and came upstairs. Then standing at the foot of my ladder he looked up at me and said "What's wrong with you two, you should have had half the ceiling done by now!" To say the least I was tired with my arms and neck aching. I was so exasperated that my first inclination was to be abusive. Instead, carefully assessing the contents of the paste bucket, I picked it up and inverted it over Dad's head. I then waited expecting him to knock me off the ladder. Yet to my great surprise he did nothing. My action had taken him completely off guard. He just stood there with paste running down his cheeks, dripping off his nose and globules dropping off his chin onto the floor. The incident was never mentioned again and we continued to work away at the redecorating until the bedrooms were finished. The ceiling was never lined - I was obviously not up to it.

Our New Home

We moved into our new home at 69, Southdown Crescent in the summer, to start my curacy in December 1975. For the first six months before this I was visiting different Churches and preaching on behalf of the South American Mission Society. I never had time to redecorate the downstairs rooms except for the hallway. Peter and Stephen were to share the back bedroom, and Deborah and Elizabeth the small one at the front. There was no study and no room for a desk so I rigged up a chipboard worktop across the bay window in our bedroom. Eddie lent me some shelves for my books, which took up the whole wall above our double bed. Fortunately the wall was extremely sturdy otherwise if we had had an earth tremor, as is common in Chile, we would have been buried in a quarter of a ton of theological tomes. George Jones, one of the Churchwardens, turned up one morning and asked "When do you expect your furniture to arrive?" I think I embarrassed him by saying we didn't have any. Anyway the question was really hypothetical because in their generosity Christ Church had fully furnished the house for the Kirk family, and they told us we had inherited all the contents. Jim Chapman was the other Churchwarden and he and Betty were very kind to us as a family inviting us to their house for tea several times. However, one grandmotherly lady puzzled me and it was my turn to be embarrassed. I happened to mention that the bedroom shared by Deborah and Elizabeth was too small. "Oh why not let them sleep in the garage?" she proffered.

Now the "garage" was at the bottom of the garden, constructed of concrete sections, with a corrugated asbestos roof, and the floor was normally covered with 3-4" of water in the winter. I suppose knowing we had been missionaries she thought we were used to primitive conditions. Or perhaps she had never seen the garage.

Another day I chatted to a Church Council member who was a Chartered Surveyor with his own business. I explained that when someone came to see me about a confidential or personal matter I had nowhere to see people in private. This didn't seem to bother him so I finally said "Would you like the idea of talking to your clients sitting on the end of your double bed?" He had nothing to say! Actually I don't think anyone had any idea how much my stipend was. In fact all our three older children were on free school dinners and my stipend was so low that I didn't pay any Income Tax. Having only recently arrived back in England we were not entitled to family allowance for the children. I believe you had to be resident in the U.K. for six months (after a period overseas) even though you had been born and lived in this country for many years.

Kindness and Generosity
Yet as I have mentioned the majority of Church members were so kind and generous. It was decided to start a house group in our home. We always started with a cup of tea or coffee. Unfortunately to our embarrassment several times we ran out of cups. However, early one morning opening the front door, there on the doorstep I found a large cardboard box full of brand new mugs. Even more generously, another morning I came down to find a manila envelope pushed through our letter box containing a hundred pounds, in ten pound notes! We never found out who these kind and generous people were. Then some weeks later I had a telephone call; after the lady had introduced herself she asked if I had an overcoat? I explained that in fact mine had been stolen in the customs in Chile. "Well I don't want to embarrass you but I have two overcoats, left by my son in law. He is an Architect living in Holland and likes to buy his new clothes in England. The coats are in very good condition, and I also have a fur coat which is surplus to requirements!" I was very pleased to accept, and then rang Bishop David Pytches, who ordained me in Chile. David was then living in Chorleywood, so he benefited from a new overcoat as well. The

4

fur coat went to a missionary wife, recently home from Paraguay, who needed a warm coat to go to her father in law's posh dinner.

Licensed by the Bishop

When the Bishop came to license me in Church it was a very informal occasion, and not during a service or anything. It involved several vows. One was allegiance to the Queen. One was to be faithful to the authority and teaching of the Bible, plus the Canons of the Church of England. Lastly I had to accept the authority of my Bishop.

I recall thinking I have no problem with these vows and am very happy to comply. My only reservation is that if any bishop expected me to do something which I considered to be contrary to the Bible's teaching I would refuse to do it. I still say to people I am an Anglican ordained in Chile - not ordained in the Church of England. There is quite a difference, as I will go on to explain later. Yet the important thing is I have no regrets on being ordained and humbly consider myself extremely honoured to be chosen to serve the Lord Jesus and know it was His purpose to ordain me. Hewlett Thompson impressed me enormously. After the licensing he came to our house to see the family. I can still him now sitting on the floor playing with the children and their toy cars. He had been a chaplain in the forces and was very much down to earth.

Elizabeth, Ann, Peter, Stephen & Deborah

The Children's Schools

Deborah and Stephen attended the Grange. They were very happy there and I would normally take Elizabeth along in the morning in her pushchair. People were always pleased to see us and greet us in the street - Elizabeth however would normally refuse to respond and I think this was shyness - but I never really knew why she did this. However both the girls made many new friends, who would come round to play at our house and also invite them to parties. In the late seventies, during the Queen's Jubilee, there were several street parties. Elizabeth entered a competition during the celebrations dressed as Britannia. I thought her costume was very good but unfortunately she didn't win a prize. Deborah however wore the same outfit in Blackheath, when we were visiting my parents. She came away with second prize just by changing the blue nightdress for a white sheet. Peter and Stephen were attired in minstrels hats and Tudor tabards when their school band played as part of the celebrations. Peter, and later Stephen, attended Whitmore High School less than half a mile from our house. During their time there they became members of the school band under the direction of Mr Denis Smith. He was a wonderful man and a committed Christian. He was also Band Master of the Wealdstone Corps of the Salvation Army. He had devised a system at Whitmore whereby the older boys would train and encourage the younger ones to become more proficient with their instruments. Peter and Stephen also joined the choir and would sing at weddings except when doing band concerts for charity with the school. They also joined Pathfinders that met on Sunday mornings with a club on Saturday evenings.

Church Services

Eddie eased me in gently so that I was never expected to lead the whole of a service at first. He would get one of the Readers to do one part and me another. I remember one day when I announced that the collection would be taken nothing happened.

Eventually from the puzzled look on people's faces I discovered I had actually spoken in Spanish! Yet there was a special bonus one week when I was due to conduct a wedding. The groom had been involved in an horrendous car crash and was left with a broken back and was unable to walk. He had spent many months in Stoke Mandeville Hospital and was attended by a very dedicated physiotherapist. She was determined to get him to walk again and consequently a romance ensued. When they decided to get married she told him he was going to walk down the aisle, which was going to be an absolute miracle. He did it and as I stood at the front, he extremely slowly but confidently walked the length of the aisle. I remember before that at the rehearsal I noticed the bride's three sisters and mother had come. The bride by the way was Colombian and spoke very good English. As the rehearsal progressed I realised that the ladies were all chatting in Spanish, and saying how delightful the Church was. So turning to the mother and addressing her in Spanish I asked where the father was? She explained that he had his own business and it was impossible for him to get away. I said "Look legally I have to conduct the vows in English. However I would be very pleased to do the prayers, plus a reading from Psalm 23, and an address in Spanish!" The mother was delighted and was consequently able to take back a recording for the bride's father in Colombia.

Pathfinders

Eddie asked me to be responsible for Pathfinders - the youngsters from age nine to thirteen. They met on a Sunday morning and had two dedicated leaders, Katherine Pritchard and Christine Swindlehurst. Over my period of three years at Christ Church the group grew in size from thirty-five to seventy. The group then became too large, so we appealed for helpers and were able to divide them up into smaller groups. We also attended several successful summer camps at Taunton, and joining with other groups was very good for us. I always remember visiting the home of a lad called Reggie. His parents couldn't afford to send him so I asked if the Church could pay for him. Wonderfully he was converted on the very Saturday morning we were due to go home. Peter and Stephen went on these camps and made some good friends in our group, some of whom also attended their school.

Excellent Tutor

Eddie was several years younger than me so frequently people thought I was the Vicar and he was the Curate. This made me smile but I was always quick to explain their mistake - though I never found out what Eddie thought about that. Eddie was very good at training me in the ways of the Church of England. He also has a very sharp mind and can read very quickly. At one stage he decided it would be good for me to go on a three day management course in London, and in fact he came as well. On the third day we were given a rapid reading test and to my astonishment I discovered that amongst forty people Eddie was the fastest reader on the course.

Eddie, of course, occasionally got rather frustrated with his new curate, especially at staff meetings. When we were discussing dates and I couldn't remember what we had agreed he'd say "Don't you keep a diary?" Or another day he said "Look in your Diary, I saw you write it down!" Eddie was an excellent preacher and teacher, whereas I would struggle with my sermons. To help me he suggested I do a series of short addresses at the early morning Communion Service. I remember that I had said to one couple that sometimes I wished the floor would open up when I was preaching. In fact I would bite my lips and felt so miserable. Then one morning something happened. That Sunday I had prepared the address in the same way and at the end of the service was walking down the aisle to go home. Eddie was to my surprise standing at the back near the entrance. As I looked at his face I could see his eyes were moist "Brother that was really good today" he said. I was rather at a loss for words so said "Well I only prepared it as I normally do." "Well," Eddie said "I suppose what was different was that I spent time in my study praying for you before the service."

Hospital Chaplain

At the side of the Church was the old Harrow Cottage Hospital and Eddie suggested we share the chaplain's responsibilities. We had two ward services on a Sunday afternoon and I encouraged several Church people to help me with these. This was mainly a geriatric hospital and here I learned from some of the young people that they found these services rather distressing. Seeing the elderly patients reminded them too much of their own grandparents. During the week I would take Communion round the wards and visit the patients. As I was visiting one afternoon an elderly patient talked with me about her two sons. Both of them had done very well, one was a chartered accountant and the other a doctor. The old lady said how good they were to her. Yet to my surprise when speaking to the ward sister she said they never visited her and hadn't been to see her for years. This made me very sad so I acquired their addresses, and wrote to them saying how pleased their mother would be to see them. This was of course against the rules and the only way I could get their addresses was when the sister was out of her office. Later to my delight I discovered (from the sister) that they had responded and had been to visit their mother.

One winter's afternoon I had been visiting the geriatric wards. Walking through one long ward all the old ladies were tightly tucked up in their beds and most seemed to be asleep. It was only about 4.00pm on a rather dark dismal day. Just before going through the fire doors a voice behind me said "You only have one life you know!"

I looked round but was unable to identify who had spoken - all of them had their heads down on their pillow. Ever since then I have never been able to forget those words. As I left the hospital and walked home down Roxeth Hill I thought "What am I so miserable about? I have a great wife and four lovely children, a job and am in perfect health. That old lady has had her life and will never come out of hospital. I have most of my life before me, so pull yourself together!" I was also reminded of some words of St Paul that came to me just before the Coup in Chile. "Make the most of the time because the days are evil." (Ephesians 5 v16.) All of us only have one life, so let's serve the Lord whilst we can, none of us know how long we are going to be on this planet.

Adoption

When we left Chile Ann had the legal guardianship of Elizabeth, so once established in Harrow we decided we must adopt her. We were appointed a lady social worker by the local council, and she would call to see us from time to time. She always made us feel nervous not knowing quite what to expect. On one occasion, when a missionary family arrived, we sent Peter off on his bike for fish and chips and the social worker turned up unexpectedly in the middle of the meal. Elizabeth had just surfaced from her afternoon nap, and not to be left out, was sitting at the end of the table with a chip in each hand! The lady, of course, asked if we always gave her chips! On another occasion she turned up the day after Elizabeth had fallen down the stairs. Although she was not badly hurt she did have a bruise on her face to our great embarrassment.

We discovered that Harrow Council was not very happy that Allende's Communist Government had been overthrown by the military. "The children should each have their own bedroom" the lady exclaimed. That was ludicrous because the Curate's house only had three bedrooms. She also said "There is too great an age gap between the children, your husband is too old and your salary is too low!" Another day she announced that Elizabeth was to be made a Ward of Court for 6 months and if Harrow Council were not satisfied with us as parents they had the power to take Elizabeth into care. At that I felt my blood rising. Ann said that I then turned to the lady and said "If you dare try to do that you can have all your files and folders back and we will catch the next plane back to Chile!"

Eventually when it came to the adoption we were advised to go to the County Court in Willesden as they would be less prejudicial. We arrived rather apprehensively, on that cold crisp morning. Elizabeth had a sore throat and wasn't feeling very well. When ushered into the judge's chambers he was sitting at a large desk. "So you've come to be adopted" he said to Elizabeth in a friendly manner. "Why not sit her on my desk" he suggested. Once on the desk she frowned at him, as she often did with strangers. He then produced two pieces of paper for us to sign and the adoption was complete. Praise the Lord the court hearing had gone through without a hitch.

Chapter 2
TIME TO MOVE

Moving On

Towards the end of three years course at Oak Hill I began to think I needed to move on. The boys would soon be studying for O levels, so would need to change schools soon, or not at all. My time with Eddie had been extremely helpful, but I began to feel there were many things I had learnt in Chile that I wanted to put into practice. This could only really be done in a Parish of my own, so I began to look in the Church of England Paper job adverts. I had also been in contact with Prebendary Arthur Royall who advised clergy who had returned from overseas. He had promised that if he felt a particular position would be suitable he would notify me. I also contacted the Church Pastoral Aid Society as they had the patronage of several Parishes.

Eddie said he very much doubted that I would get a Living, and in any case I had to convince the authorities that I wouldn't suddenly up sticks and return to Chile. First I was offered a further Curacy in North London and later CPAS came up with a Parish in Streatham Hill. The latter Church building needed a new roof so didn't really attract me. Then there was the possibility of a Team Vicar's post in the St Paul's area of Bristol. I went for an interview and the Rector was very keen for me to take the job. However the main problem was it was in an area where the ladies of the night plied their trade in the street outside the Vicarage and we had four children. Sadly, I also discovered that a previous Vicar had committed suicide. Again, I really didn't feel it was a challenge I was prepared to tackle.

Job Interviews

Then I saw a Parish advertised in Nottinghamshire so I wrote asking for an interview. CPAS also contacted me regarding a Church in Newcastle. Later I was intrigued to discover that a Chilean Petty Officer, who was worshipping at this Church, had seen my name on a list at the CPAS office and recommended me. Juan Valenzuela was living in the area awaiting the refit of a Naval destroyer to sail back to Chile. We had previously worked together at Church summer camps in the Valparaiso area.

Within a few days I was called for an interview for the Jesmond Dene Parish. The trustees very generously paid the return rail fare for Ann and myself. The meeting was held in a very impressive building on the waterfront in Newcastle where the Chairman had his office. To my surprise at the end of the interview they offered me the Living and gave me fourteen days to make my decision. I needed to explain however that I was waiting for an interview for another a Parish. Whilst in Newcastle Ann and I did go to see the Vicarage but found it really unsuitable, especially bearing in mind the children as it had virtually no garden.

The Nottinghamshire interview soon came through as Prebendary Royall had actually passed on my details to the trustees. The Patron telephoned suggesting the interview be held in St James Park, London, knowing we were living in Harrow. Again I took Ann with me as I always felt it was necessary that she had the chance to ask any questions that were important to her. Arriving at what appeared to be a firm of solicitors we entered their offices. We were then ushered into a large capacious room, with a large leather sofa and armchairs. As we waited Ann soon noticed a familiar well worn brief case, and rain coat thrown over a chair. "I bet I know who those things belong to!" Ann exclaimed. Within a few minutes we could hear someone coming down the stairs, the door opened and to my amazement Arthur Robinson appeared. He was a friend whom we had worked with in Chile. "You're next" he said with a slight smile! Then just before leaving Arthur said "I've decided not to be considered. I've already visited the Parish and find I could never work with the present Parish hierarchy!"

The Patron, with two other trustees, faced Ann and myself across a large desk. Of course I was nervous, but I was absolutely astounded for within a few minutes he asked "What is your experience of the Holy Spirit?" As I reflect on this I am still amazed to think that the Patron of a Church of England Parish should ask such a question. Yet it was tailor made for me. I was able to tell of how Chilean believers prayed for me expecting Jesus to fulfil His promise that His disciples would speak in new tongues (Mark 16 v17). Then how the Holy Spirit motivated me (after many months of struggling) to learn Spanish. Of how Chilean Christians, both Anglicans and Pentecostals, taught me to expect miracles. For they knew Jesus had taught His disciples to expect them, and to lay hands on the sick to receive healing. Eventually when the interview ended I was delighted to be offered the Living. I later discovered from Roy Wilson, Rector of Ripley, he had been praying for me with John Wright, the Patron. I think they had been at a conference and took time out to pray for me.

Next, after the interview, I needed to get up to Nottinghamshire to see the Parish. We had been praying for a "Mission field in England", and this seemed to be the Lord's answer. Leaving the interview room we went straight to a public telephone to ring Newcastle to say I would not be coming to Jesmond Dene. I was sorry in many ways, yet convinced the Lord wanted me in Nottinghamshire. Of course the other very important factor was that the Parish in Nottinghamshire would be nearer to my parents in London.

Chapter 3
NEW PARISH

Visit to New Parish

Getting home I quickly rang the present Incumbent to arrange a visit. He was soon to retire and very graciously invited me to stay overnight saying "I'm looking forward to meeting you and will be happy to answer any questions." A few days later however I was shocked to receive a call from the Patron saying not to go as the Vicar had died very suddenly. The Parish was of course in a great state of shock, principally because they were planning all the arrangements for his retirement just before Easter. However a few days later one of the Churchwardens was kind enough to let me stay there. The Bishop asked us not to go to the Vicarage as this might cause the widow distress. Surprisingly she then sent word saying she would like to meet us and kindly offered us some furniture, which we were pleased to accept.

In the meantime Arthur had written giving me his assessment of the Parish. On arrival I discovered to my amazement that I was looking at the biggest Churchyard I have ever seen. As I was walking around the back of the Church I was suddenly surprised by Eric whom I later discovered was the gravedigger. "Are you going to be our new Vicar?" he asked. At that stage I didn't want to say much, yet later I found him to be extremely supportive and we became great friends.

I really wanted to meet the Church Council and mentioned this to the Bishop. He was not very keen and said "Well I don't like PCCs interviewing my clergy!"

However I did and at the end of the meeting I asked if anyone had any questions. One lady, who was a retired schoolteacher, asked me "Do you allow lay people to do readings in the services?" I was rather surprised because in all the Churches I knew members of the congregation always did. So I replied "Yes of course, I would be pleased to." I noticed amongst the gathered assembly a couple of young men in their middle thirties. I could see leadership potential there and in fact they later went on to be Churchwardens and eventually ordained. I don't remember any embarrassing or difficult questions and the meeting seemed to go off well. But I began to think this place feels a bit like Rip Van Winkle's land, it seems to have been left behind in a time warp.

Sadly my father went into hospital a few days before we moved to Nottingham. He was very jaundiced and they discovered he had another cancer, this time of the pancreas. He had already looked up train and coach timetables, and he was so looking forward to seeing me inducted in my own Parish in England. My parents were so proud, and as always so supportive. Dad however died just a few days before my induction, so we came back for the funeral at St John's, Blackheath where we had grown up. Later we were to bring my mother up to Nottinghamshire, she had always lived in the same area of London all her life. So at eighty she came to live in a small bungalow in a road just behind the Vicarage, where the children could pop round to see her every day.

Friday Night and Breakdown Night

We drove up one Friday evening in our old Vauxhall Viva a few days before my induction. The Motorway was very busy and we saw several private cars broken down. Suddenly it became our turn - I can't remember exactly what the trouble was - but we pulled over onto the hard shoulder. Not having any breakdown cover I decided to walk up to the next services which were not very far.

The car was well loaded of course, with Ann and myself, four children, plus a gerbil in a cage, the gold fish in a bowl, and goodness knows what else all in the back. I was afraid to leave the family in the car so creating a crocodile we all trudged up to the services. Speaking to the mechanics they then told me I was breaking the law, and should remain in the car. I ignored them because it was a dark miserable night and my main concern was for the children's safety.

I can't remember all the details, but they couldn't help me and so a breakdown vehicle was called. We hung around to be eventually told our car could not be repaired, as they hadn't got the spares. Actually I discovered that the mechanic was at a party.

Anyway we were told to go home and ring up later. "How do I do that then?" I asked. They then came up with the idea of calling a local taxi firm. Fortunately I had the telephone number one of the Churchwardens, so eventually Alan very kindly came to the rescue. We rang up on Saturday but the car was still not ready, so eventually they notified us we could collect it on Sunday afternoon. This time Stanley, the other Churchwarden, kindly took me down to collect the car on Sunday afternoon.

Induction

At my Induction some people thought it rather strange that two Bishops were in attendance. One was of course the Diocesan Bishop Denis Wakelin, the other was Bishop David Pytches. David had ordained me in Chile and has always been very supportive. Rev Eddie Shirras, my Vicar in Harrow, came up with a coach full of people from London. After the service the coach got a bit lost trying to find the Parish Hall. The reception was fantastic, if that's the right word. I shall never forget on entering the Hall being immediately greeted by two enormous turkeys. All the massive amount of food immediately demonstrated the generosity and joyful welcome the parishioners had in receiving their new Incumbent.

I must now make my confession concerning two incidents that occurred causing great consternation. John and Sally Patrick (some friends from Blackheath) were returning to London following a camping holiday in the Lake District. Unfortunately during the journey they lost their tent off the roof rack of the car with most of their camping equipment and so were delayed. Arriving late they went straight to the Vicarage only to discover that no one was at home and it was all locked up. John, an experienced climber and taking the initative, clambered up onto the porch and found a bedroom window open. Once inside he opened the front door so he and Sally could quickly get their small children to bed. I must say that this had unfortunately not gone unnoticed!

During the Church service at one point the new Incumbent had to ring the bell. The Tower Captain had carefully extended a length of rope down from the belfry so that the new man could toll the bell. According to tradition the number of times the bell was rung indicated the number of years the new Vicar would stay in the Parish. I can't remember exactly now but after pulling the rope six or seven times it suddenly became unhitched and I found myself entangled in yards and yards of rope. I was, to say the least, uncertain what to do next. Now at this the Patricks, who were standing quite near to me, became overwhelmed with fits of laughter! Again this had not gone unnoticed and one senior Churchman was greatly upset at "the outrageous behaviour of these yobs!" What he didn't realise was that John was a kidney consultant and he and his wife had been working with a Christian charity amongst the poor people in the West Indies.

At one of our first meetings the Churchwardens asked me to reassure them that I would not make any changes during my first year and I agreed. There were two services at the Parish Church – the early morning Prayer

Book Communion at 9.00am with no sermon. Quite different from Harrow where there was always a short sermon, as the Prayer Book calls for. In the evening was a Prayer Book service led by a robed choir where the most important feature seemed to the "The day Thou gavest" always sung at the cross aisle.

Chapter 4
END OF HONEYMOON PERIOD

Promised Curate Causes Crisis

Originally the Bishop had said I could have another Curate, which I was very much looking forward to. I was extremely grateful but asked if I might wait until I had been in the Parish for a year. Thus giving me time to assess what work I would assign to him. Later it seemed that what we most needed was someone to especially concentrate on working with young teenagers. He could also share in the large number of funerals, weddings and pastoral work. Unfortunately when the idea of a Curate was raised it was soon to cause considerable unrest amongst the hierarchy. Their main concern seemed to be a financial one. Realising there was a storm gathering I contacted the Archdeacon, who came to talk with the Churchwardens and Standing Committee. After the meeting he told me "You'll be all right now John, they seem to be assured and have agreed to the idea." However, returning to the dining room to my astonishment the group then rounded on me and said "This Curate is the Vicar's idea - we have always paid our quota and if this goes ahead we shall struggle to pay our way!" I think it was about this time that the Lord first brought to my mind a phrase in Isaiah 8 verse 12 "Do not fear what they fear". Important words which would come to me over and over again during the years ahead.

Churchwardens Resign

Two days later one of the Churchwardens came to the Vicarage to say they were writing to the Bishop. They were furious and weren't going to put up with the way things were going. "Can you drop a copy of the letter through my letter box please, so I can defend myself?" I requested. "Oh, you'll find out soon enough when you get summoned to see the Bishop" came the reply, and turning round he walked away. They were in determined mood and wanted to get me out at all costs!

When I was called to see the Bishop I was ushered into his office and he invited me to sit down. Leaning back in his chair and holding up the letter he said "Well there's a great head of steam here!" Then later he added, "What I shall do is delay your Curate's coming, to give things a chance to cool down a bit. His Vicar has been ill for several months so I shall wait until he is either better, or a new man is appointed." So it eventually transpired that David's arrival was delayed for over a year.

Unbelievably a few days later, when the Bishop was due to come for a Confirmation Service, the Churchwardens resigned. The Bishop responded saying that with the AGM soon due they should stand down then, and not seek re-election. But they were adamant and refused to comply. I really didn't know what to do next! Then quickly thumbing through my Churchwardens Handbook I discovered you could appoint wardens just for the occasion, as a temporary measure. So after prayer I nominated Grace Lindley and Nora Langton as Churchwardens with Ernie Hill and Cecil Butler as deputies.

Curate Saga Continues

I continued to pray about the Curate situation. Eventually I felt all was not lost and thought at least we could set up a fund for his rent and expenses - the Bishop had said the diocese would pay his stipend. So I opened a building society account and invited people to contribute. I was soon so encouraged and delighted by people's generosity, for within three months we had received at least £1,400, which would accrue interest until he came. Although on the negative side we still had a couple of acrimonious Church Council meetings. At one of these Ann suggested that to pay the Curate's costs "Some of us young mums could chip in with an amount equivalent to our family allowance." This caused one senior Church member to react angrily saying "That's illegal, and would get into the local press giving the Church a bad name!" Such a response was completely unreasonable and deliberately misconstrued Ann's intentions. At this she burst into tears and immediately left the meeting. As she was leaving Church our small daughter Elizabeth asked "Why are you crying Mummy?" This was the last PCC meeting Ann would attend as I asked her to resign. In the future Ann would stay at home with the children. I was so hurt, why should my wife be subjected to such acrimony and unkindness.

Chapter 5
PASTORAL VISITING

Some people I met in Pastoral visiting

Of course in the beginning I had plenty of visiting to do. "Would you call to see an old lady who can't get out and about much these days?" I was asked one day. I was happy to do that, so arriving at the house I walked round to the back door. I had discovered that most people didn't use the front door, and this was apparent by the weeds on the step and sometimes lack of paint on the woodwork. Also, that it was considered unlucky if you entered one door and left by another. Once the lady had opened the door she ushered me through into the front room. She soon gave me a cup of tea, but remained standing and seemed rather anxious about something.

"You seem worried" I said, and waited for her to respond. "Well I have a problem with my washing machine and its stopped going!" she blurted out. "Would you like me to look at it? I don't pretend to know much about washing machines?" I said.

So going through to the kitchen I found an old fashioned top loading machine. Looking inside it was absolutely full, and seemed to have an old raincoat wrapped around the spindle. It didn't seem to have a mechanical fault to me, so I asked her if the raincoat was one her husband still used? "Well it's very old and doesn't really matter too much" she said. So finally asking her for a pair of scissors I proceeded to cut away the guilty garment. At once the machine began to function and the old lady was delighted. Later a friend asked her "What do you think of the new Vicar then?" "Oh I think he's a wonderful man, he actually repaired my washing machine!" she replied. That wasn't really correct but it was good for my image, and an excellent report was put around the village.

Another morning I received a phone call from a lady who also wanted to meet the new Vicar. Arriving at the door I knocked twice and eventually she came to the door. She was in her late seventies and was housebound but soon invited me in, asking if I would like a cup of tea. "Please sit down while I put the kettle on - I won't be a few minutes" she said. As I sat there in front of me was a small coffee table with a bowl of nuts on. So as I waited I began to help myself. Coming back with the tea she seemed a little surprised to see I was eating the nuts, and exclaimed "Oh I see you are making yourself at home - actually those nuts used to be covered in chocolate but I sucked it all off!" She then asked me through to the front room and here was another surprise. On the dining table she had between thirty and forty prayer cards from different missionaries all over the world. She was a fantastic prayer warrior and prayed regularly for them all. "I always attended the little chapel down the road" she said. "But sadly it closed, and now these days I find it so difficult to get out and about."

Amongst the people I used to visit regularly was another very committed lady in her late seventies. Although she and her husband were quite elderly she had a very active Christian faith. Many years ago the couple had worked for the then Vicar the Rev Charles Harrison. She had been the maid and her husband the gardener. I enjoyed these visits, when the bone china cups and saucers were brought out, and she served me with tea and cakes. It was just like visiting an old aunt. But for me the thing I most appreciated was our spiritual conversations, and our time of prayer when she always prayed for me. One day she confessed the great sadness she had because her husband never prayed with her. "If he only said the Lords Prayer at night with me I would be so encouraged" she said. Her husband's health was failing and they were such a devoted couple. Then one day she shared with me some joyful news. Her husband had actually started to say the Lord's Prayer with her in the evenings. A few days later he died, but the Lord had answered her prayers.

There was also a lovely old gentleman I enjoyed visiting who lived in the sheltered flats at St Helen's Court. He was in his nineties and was completely bedridden.

He was another great prayer warrior who loved to sit up in bed and praise the Lord lifting his arms above his head. I discovered he wasn't an Anglican, but a member of the Pentecostal Church, and always prayed for me when I went to see him.

Chapter 6
STRANGE THINGS HAPPEN

Series of Strange Scenarios

After the Churchwardens had resigned over the few next months or so a series of strange things happened. On several occasions just before a funeral our organist Oswald Smith (with whom I got on very well) reported the organ wasn't working. I had no idea what caused the problem but eventually Ossie and I discovered that each time the fuse to the organ had been taken out!

The second occurrence happened when the deputy head of the Church of England School asked if the children could come into Church to practice for a carol service.

This was the first time the school had come into Church since my appointment so I was extremely pleased to cooperate. The piano was tucked away behind a pillar so the lady asked me if it could be moved, as she needed it closer to the front enabling her to see the children over the top. The piano was a very heavy instrument. So the two of us struggled to get it down two stone steps into a better position. Despite this the rehearsal went well and I looked forward to seeing the children come the next time. However, going into Church the following week we couldn't find the piano! It had mysteriously gone back behind the pillar. Each time the children came for their practice this was repeated, yet we never found out how! In fact one year Bishop David Pytches announced at the New Wine Conference "I have a friend who had to get a faculty to move the piano." In case the term is unfamiliar this is a special legal document granted by the Diocese for permission to make structural alterations to the Church building.

Thirdly in the early 1980's there was a scheme in Nottinghamshire to get more trees planted. I was happy to go along with that so some new trees were planted. Around that time Manpower Services came with a gang of people to cut the grass and clear the rubbish in our very large Churchyard. Then one morning quite unexpectedly a Churchwarden came to the Vicarage, he had discovered a number of young trees had been cut down. Why would anyone want to do that? Some people assumed I had given orders to the Manpower Services foreman to do it, but he affirmed most definitely I had not. It was also reported in the local press, I therefore have the strong feeling that someone was trying to embarrass me.

During my first two years in the Parish other Churches and friends would ring up to ask "How are things going in the Parish"? With such strange things going on all I could say was "Well it feels like being dragged through a hedge backwards!" Which is why I thought this was perhaps the best title for the book! I just didn't know what was happening. I was bewildered and not knowing who to go to for help or advice. But I knew some people in our own Deanery, and others from Churches further afield, were praying for us, and the Lord was answering those prayers. One Incumbent in our Deanery (born and bred in Nottinghamshire) would often ask facetiously "How are you getting on with taming the natives?"

Chapter 7
INFANT BAPTISM

A Blockage with Baptisms

The most difficult policy I managed to put into practice was one on infant Baptism. Soon after my induction I decided to study the Church registers. Of course this was something I should have done before, as probably a more experienced clergyman would have done. Indeed with hindsight it might even have caused me to seriously doubt that I should take the Parish. As I looked through the Baptism Register I discovered to my astonishment that something approaching six hundred infants had been baptised in the last few years. But not one of these families ever came to Church after the baptism, as I would have expected them to. Of course there is nearly always a backlog of people waiting for baptisms where there has been an interregnum. So I cleared these but then began to think about what we should be doing here.

The Canons stipulate that I could not refuse to baptise any infant living in my Parish. But it was in order to delay baptism where the parents needed teaching regarding the meaning of the Christian faith. So I began by asking parents and godparents to come to the Vicarage for two preparation classes. I also asked these families to begin to attend at least one or two Family Services which included a baptism. For amongst the promises in the service comes the question "Will you help your child to take their place within the life and worship of Christ's Church?" The two sets of promises regarding the rejection of evil, renouncing deceit and corruption, and repentance for sin are of extreme importance. As are those promises about the need to "Turn to Christ as Saviour and submitting to Him as Lord." My friend Peter Thurston (who had been a former CMS missionary) told me he wanted to impress upon parents the seriousness of these promises. So he used to say to parents if they were to make such promises in a court of law, and then not keep them, they would be in danger of perjuring themselves!

I also began to discourage private baptisms as the Canons of the Church of England and the Prayer Book say that baptisms should take place when the most number of people come together. Unfortunately members of the Royal Family without fail continue to have private baptisms, which set a bad example. Why not have these baptisms take place in Westminster Abbey so we could all see them? We could then have them televised!

In the main I would not be too strict if parents were not confirmed, if they had a reasonable understanding of Christianity. Parents often believed that if their daughter had not been baptised she could not be married in Church. I quickly explained that was not the case. Some even believed that if you were not baptised you could not be given a Christian funeral in Church. Again I needed to correct that. Sadly I discovered from some in the Parish that one mother never even asked me to baptise her child because he was disabled! Presumably thinking I might refuse! Most families however complied with the baptism preparation sessions. One exception came when the telephone rang and an irate great grandmother gave me a good ear bashing. Realising I had previously been a missionary she bellowed "We understand all about baptism, you are not dealing with ignorant savages now you know!" I never had the opportunity to meet the old lady and discovered later she was actually housebound. The great granddaughter never came to see me and I can't remember what the final outcome was. On some occasions a whole family, plus godparents, would come to the Vicarage. There could be as many as seventeen people turn up, and as I ushered them into our lounge you could sense the hostility. They assumed they would encounter some objection on my part, or as one person said "I was sure you would set up further hurdles to the baptism."

One Sunday morning crossing the road I slipped on the grass verge and got myself all plastered with mud. I was due to lead the Family Service and knew I would be late for I had been forced to change my clothes and was rushing back to Church. A young mum was standing by the Vicarage gate with a pushchair and I smiled as I sped past. Many months later I discovered she wanted to ask about a baptism and said I was too busy to speak to her!

As time went on when I received a baptism enquiry I would go to visit the family. This would give me an opportunity to spend time with them in the relaxed environment of their own home and get to know them.

Here I would like to include something I still remember quite vividly when two ladies turned up at the Vicarage one Monday morning. I wasn't in so Ann invited them in to wait. Ann, in fact, was in the midst of sorting out the family washing, and had loads of dirty clothes set out in piles all around our large kitchen table. The ladies had come to make an enquiry about a baptism. Stephanie had Fran with her presumably to give her a bit of moral support. Ann was just thinking of offering them a cup of coffee when Stephen appeared in the kitchen only dressed in his underpants, looked very embarrassed and started raiding the fridge. Ann immediately turned round and told him off for cutting such a large lump of cheese. The ladies however were absolutely flabbergasted because they had never seen such a scenario before - I suppose thinking that Vicar's wives didn't do that sort of thing! Months later, when we got to know Stephanie better she told us she was really surprised to find that we, like them, had dirty laundry and kids that needed yelling at! After the baptism Stephanie and Alan began regularly attending the Family Services. Eventually Stephanie felt that the Lord was calling her to take over the leadership of Guides. Later Alan found that he and I had a mutual interest in the Boys Brigade and so he became an officer in a local company.

A Breakthrough with Baptisms

The Anglican Incumbent from an adjoining Parish (with whom I prayed regularly) was also very disturbed by the general culture in our communities concerning baptism. Actually his mother was from Panama and his father was American. So this probably made him reflect on the way Baptism is done in Latin America. After a short time in his Parish he discovered that when a person gave their life to Christ they wanted to be baptised. The problem was that some of them didn't know whether they had been baptised as infants or not. Julio Bustos, one of the students on placement with me from St John's

Elizabeth Joyce Tew
Baptised 26th June 1982

College, was also concerned with this dilemma. As an ordained Anglican Minister from Chile, Julio knew that because of this problem these people often felt they had missed out on an important part of the Christian faith. To see adults being baptised you realised what an important thing this ceremony was. As you saw candidates being totally immersed and then coming up out of the water you realised they were making their own personal public declaration of their commitment to Christ. This event was something they would never forget for the rest of their lives. Surely this was the way Jesus' disciples and St Paul had carried out baptisms in the New Testament. Going under the water and coming up again symbolises our dying to sin and being raised to new life in Christ (Romans 6 v4). There is a verse that always sticks in my mind about baptism and this is the command Jesus gave to His disciples in Mark 16 verse 16 "Whoever believes and is baptised will be saved, but whoever does not believe will be condemned."

Of course the Church of England's Book of Common Prayer includes a service of thanksgiving for the birth of a child called "The Churching of Women." So in the early days I invited families to come into Church for that before baptism. Later I began to use the service of "Thanksgiving for the Birth of a Child" during the Family Service, with a certificate for the parents published by St John's College, Bramcote. The certificate says this should be given to the Minister when the child is baptised. Later the Incumbent, with whom I prayed regularly, gave adults the chance to take part in a service of renewal of baptismal vows. For this he would use a baptistery and take candidates down into the water to give them the experience of being baptised by total immersion. This greatly interested me but was something I never had the courage to do myself. Although later I did begin baptising a number of new Christians by total immersion in an Anglican Church in Hucknall where there was a baptistery. On some occasions I also used the baptistery in the local Church of Christ.

Gradually as time passed more families began to attend Church services after their children had been baptised. Following our policy, and the preparation classes, people were beginning to understand that baptism was about commitment to Christ and growing in discipleship. Eventually the day came when these families started asking me for a regular mid-morning service every week. No longer was the Church suffering from smaller attendances, but rejoicing because of a growth in numbers, and I will relate more about that later.

Chapter 8
WALKING OVER THE WATER

One day, quite early on during my time in the Parish, one of the Churchwardens alerted me to the fact that we seemed to be using a lot of water. The storage tank was in the vestry, and opening the cupboard door we heard the noise of continually running water. It was difficult to see inside but we were losing gallons of water every day and we had a leak somewhere. We checked the tap in the Churchyard and the washbasin in the outside toilet. It would seem we had a leak on the central heating system. We walked around the interior of the Church and could find no evidence of any leak. We had a serious and expensive problem.

One of the Churchwardens contacted the water board knowing that they had sophisticated microphones that could detect leaks underground. In the end they replied they were only responsible for pipes outside Church boundaries and couldn't help us. I rang several heating firms that had done work in Churches around the diocese. They came up with the answer that if we dug up the floor and found the leak they would carry out the repair free of charge. But where did we start? I was so worried as each time I went into the vestry I could hear the water running ceaselessly.

Eventually a group of us decided to go into Church and tackle the problem. I continued to pray "Lord where do we start?" We agreed to meet in Church at 6.30pm and one Churchwarden came armed with some drain rods. When I came in I found the group waiting and someone asked me "Where do we start Vicar?" My heart sank "Lord where?" I prayed again quietly. I eventually glanced across the Church towards the South Aisle near the front. As I looked my eyes alighted on a large Viking pipe connection where there had been a repair some months before. That wasn't leaking but there was still a hole in the floor, which had not been filled in. So summoning the little confidence I had I said "Try putting a rod down there into the pipe duct." My idea was to see if it came out wet - it didn't. "Put another rod on with a rag wrapped around it and try again please" I said nervously. Just one more try I thought. This time to my utter amazement the rag came out wet! The place was immediately under the lectern. We quickly cut up the ceramic tiles and there was the leak. The rusty iron pipe (some inch and a half in diameter) was completely severed. We stood and watched as gallons and gallons of water were being pumped out of the pipe. Where the water was going we didn't know, presumably it was running away under the Church somewhere.

Soon after the small group dispersed with Fred Slater and myself being the only ones left. I locked the Church door and we walked down the path crossing the road to the Vicarage. I was about to say "good night" when Fred said "I'm ashamed of you John!" I was rather puzzled "Why?" I asked. He replied "Well I thought surely you will say let's pray, praising the Lord for such a marvellous answer to prayer!" Fred was absolutely right so we gave thanks there and then in our gateway. Some days later the heating firm came and repaired the broken pipe. They were as good as their word and would not take any payment. We had been walking over the water for weeks and had no idea where it had all been going - supposedly under the Church somewhere.

Chapter 9
BOUQUETS AND BRICKBATS

Continuing Discontent

I remember one evening in my early years, when we were going to a meeting of the Deanery Synod with the Churchwardens. The most important item on the agenda was of course finance. The object was to complain that our quota was too high.

Among other things discussed in the car was that people were paying me compliments. One of the Churchwardens immediately blurted out "Now you've had the bouquets here's some brickbats." I fail to remember what they were but brickbats were often the order of the day in the first few years. Nearly every Sunday evening the wardens or senior Church members came into the vestry just before the service with complaints. I would always try to listen carefully in case they had a point. But afterwards I used to feel absolutely drained and consequently found it very hard to get motivated to lead the service and preach afterwards. Fortunately this all changed after the wardens resigned and the new ones were appointed. It was then so refreshing as they would come to pray with me in the vestry before the service. I remember when I was at All Nations College in 1966 and preaching at different Churches, especially the Free Churches, the deacons always prayed with the Minister before the service. Later in my own Parish I realised that complaints would still come in, but we would deal with those at some other time.

One Sunday after the new Churchwardens had been appointed there was an unfortunate argument at the Church door following the evening service. I think an older member had complained because we had sung a different tune to one of the hymns, and was arguing with a Churchwarden. People were trying to leave Church but this heated dispute was blocking the way. When I realised what was going on I walked down the Church and said "Look why don't we go over to the Vicarage now, you are spoiling the whole atmosphere after the service, let's discuss this over a cup of coffee.!" When the objector declined I finally said "The Churchwardens are my officers and I support them fully, so if you have a valid complaint have it out with me."

My family had to cope with complaints as well. Peter's first job was with a local engineering firm, where he was very fortunate to get an apprenticeship. One thing he was expected to do was deliver small engineering parts to customers. He had been out one evening and his car had broken down. It's possible that I had to tow him home: to be truthful I can't remember now. However he had to get his car ready for work on Monday and the repair meant taking the engine out. Being a big undertaking he worked all day Saturday and through Sunday. That evening he was almost finished and was up to his eyeballs in grease. The evening service had just finished in Church and one of the older members came across the road. Addressing my son he said "Why didn't you go to Church tonight then?" Peter told me later he could sense his blood rising, but he controlled his anger. "What has your Church got to offer me?" he responded. Which I must say was quite a reasonable thing to say. Unhappily this event made my son finally decide to stop coming to Church.

In Harrow there was a flourishing Youth Fellowship for youngsters of his age - but here there was nothing! The old man couldn't answer Peter so turned and walked away.

Another time the same old gentleman wanted to know why my sons didn't help with clearing the snow from the Church path? He had the idea that my family was part of my unpaid staff. This really rankled me as I thought you have two grandsons of a similar age why don't you ask them? I found the old man's attitude so depressing, lacking in understanding, and made me extremely angry. His approach was to keep my sons occupied by giving them jobs to do. Obviously what was needed was a youth programme, but it was going to be several years before that was to happen. By which time, very sadly, it was too late for Peter and Stephen!

However the Lord did provide other activities. On the positive side there was a brass band at Kirkby. Both boys had been very much impressed with the local Salvation Army in Chile. Whilst at school in Harrow the two of them had been in the band there, so the Kirkby Welfare Miners

Kirkby Miners Welfare Band

Band was literally a godsend! Once enrolled Stephen played tuba and Peter euphonium. From time to time they went on band tour and made lots of friends, many of their own age with a number attending their local secondary school. Stephen eventually went on to join the Territorial Army Band, and finally signed on with the Royal Corps of Signals.

More recently John Cheese told me "We once asked Stephen what he was going to do when he was in the Army?" To which Stephen replied "Well I'm going to shoot 'em and my Dad's going to bury them!" Stephen later had several tours in Northern Ireland and was blown up by the I.R.A. Praise God he was not seriously injured. Then in 1991 he was sent to Iraq and once again came home safely.

Fortunately things were different for the girls. Deborah joined the bell ringers, and Elizabeth later joined Sparklers. Deborah was also able to join the Youth Fellowship when that began later.

The Parish Magazine and the Bible
One job the Vicar was expected to do was edit the Parish Magazine (something I had never done before!) I had a great desire to persuade people to read the Bible, and so one month I included an article on the value of Bible reading. A few days after the magazine was published one of the older Church members came to the Vicarage.

"Where did that stuff about reading the Bible come from?" he demanded. He went on to say "I mean what good have you done for our Church since you've been here?"

I took it on the chin and said nothing. Yet to my amazement a few days later I had a phone call "I'm ringing to ask if I could use your article about Bible reading in my own Church magazine. I don't live in your Parish but I found it really helpful?"

The other thing that encouraged me about this time was when a generous lady gave me a donation to provide for our first set of pew Bibles in Church, as we had never had any before. I was also keen to include things in the magazine that showed the relevance of Christianity in people's lives. I longed to get people to share their experiences of how the Lord had answered prayer or encouraged them. So at one stage Linda took on the task of speaking to people and interviewing them to get their testimonies. Of course sometimes we struggled to get enough material for the magazine, although at other times we had too much!

Chapter 10
MOTHERLY SUPPORT

Mothers' Union

Mothers' Union Outing
Sheila Ingham, Betty Wigman, Grace Lindley,
Joan Barsby, Marion Warner

From the beginning under the leadership of Grace Lindley the Mothers Union went well. It was a sizeable group and their meetings were always well attended and I was invited to preside at a Communion Service at regular intervals. They also arranged some interesting speakers and went on outings. They were so loyal, encouraging me and were really supportive. Asked to speak at a Deanery event I began with the question "What do you think is the most important union of all?"

I was, of course, referring to our union with Christ. On another occasion I was asked to lead a quiet afternoon. After a short address I suggested they divide into small groups to pray. As I watched, some ladies from another Church near the front just sat and talked. So I eventually asked them "Aren't you going to pray?"

Slightly surprised they said "Oh we've never done that before, nobody has shown us!"

After some time in the Parish it seemed a good idea if we could serve a cup of tea following the evening service. This would be a bit of a challenge because we had no facilities. We of course mentioned what was going to happen during the notices. The best place to serve tea seemed to be under the Tower, and two faithful members of the Mothers' Union very bravely fixed up a small boiler, electric kettle, and set out cups and saucers on trays. However, sadly when the time came after the service, most members of the congregation just ignored the ladies and went straight home. Others made disparaging remarks. One person said "This is like Littlewoods café on Saturday afternoon!" Hearing about this I immediately left the vestry, without taking off my robes, and walked down to the back of the Church. I was so disappointed and sad as when I got there I found the two gallant ladies in tears! Determined to encourage them I said "Oh please don't be put off I would love a cup of tea, and I'll see if I can get others to have one too!" However, praise the Lord, this was not the last time that tea was served in Church, and eventually the idea was accepted.

Later, coming up to my retirement, I asked Grace if the Mothers' Union could help take Communion round to our local nursing homes. Again something never done before, but a small group including Sheila Ingham took on the task. There were four nursing homes in the Parish, including one at Jacksdale and the St Helen's Court sheltered flats. This went well, so I arranged that when I eventually retired they would ask the Rev Ernie Hill to consecrate the elements, and the residents would continue to receive their monthly Communion during the interregnum.

Chapter 11
THINKING OF ORDINATION

Non-Stipendiary Minister

I had only been in the Parish a short while when Ernie Hill asked to come and see me.

Ernie had been born and bred in the community, had been Sunday School Superintendent, Churchwarden and a Reader for seventeen years. This was one of our early meetings so he said "What do we call you Vicar?" I tried not to be surprised and responded "Well I wasn't baptised Vicar was I, call me John!" So we soon began a great friendship.

Ernie said he had this feeling that perhaps God was calling him to be ordained. He was hesitant because, as he said, he had not been to university and had worked most of his life in a factory. I could see where he was coming from, but he had proved his potential over the years. So I remember saying "Well Ernie let's go for it!" He was put on a selection course, and later the Director of Ordinands rang me to say Ernie had been accepted. He went on to do his training at St John's College, Bramcote, which consisted of a part time course plus written assignments as he was still at work during the week.

Eventually when it came to his ordination retreat Bishop Denis Wakeling had just retired. Ernie was somewhat concerned about this, and wondered if his ordination might be postponed. Richard Darby, the Suffragan Bishop, was however most positive and during Ernie's retreat said "Look Ernie I'm going to ordain you, because I want you ordained!"

Ernie's ordination was indeed a watershed for he became the first Local Non Stipendiary Minister in the Southwell Diocese. Later he was upgraded to Non-Stipendiary Minister, which meant he could serve in the wider Church anywhere. In the future, amongst other responsibilities, he became Chaplain to the Royal

Rev Ernie & Jean Hill ordained at Southwell
(1987)

British Legion. Consequently people would often ring me to ask "Mr Jacklin would it be possible for the Rev Hill to do my daughter's wedding?" I had no problem with that at all because everybody knew Ernie and respected him, whereas I had only been around for a little while. In fact we asked Ernie to officiate at our daughter Elizabeth's wedding, and as someone said "Ernie did it with his usual aplomb!"

Chapter 12
CHAPLAINCY AND POSSIBLE PASTORATES

Barcelona

Wanting to use my Spanish I offered to do a locum for the Chaplain at St George's Barcelona. It came at a hectic period when we were having lots of funerals and I felt that in some ways "a change was as good as a rest". By this time my son Peter had started his first job but to my disappointment Stephen decided he wasn't interested in the chance to practice his Spanish. I remember that at the time I was so tired and stressed I nearly called the whole thing off. However, eventually travelling with the two girls we journeyed by car and finally carried the vehicle across France by train to Lyon. From there we drove the car for the last 60 miles to Barcelona. The Chaplain's flat was over the Church and I was expected to do a couple of services each Sunday, plus pastoral visiting during the week. St. George's is a very light, airy and modern building. In contrast it's interesting to know that in Spain most protestant Churches are very dark inside with few windows, as many were attacked as part of the persecution during the civil war.

Early one morning there was a phone call from London for the Chaplain, getting us out of bed. Later the lady pastoral assistant contacted me saying the American Fleet had arrived to do manoeuvres with the Spanish fleet, and I was expected to go down to the port to welcome them. "Why can't you go down?" I asked, but she said it had to be the Chaplain. However it was such a surprising and encouraging experience to meet with the Rev Ralph Gibson, a Baptist minister who was their Chaplain. He told me he was on a short-term commission, as he had felt the Lord calling him to work in the navy for three years. How, that through a weekly Bible study a group of eight sailors had been converted on the Aircraft Carrier. These were voluntary meetings held below decks just sitting on packing cases. There was also another vessel alongside that turned out to be a supply ship called the Saratoga. I then remembered we had seen these ships before whilst Ann and I were on the beach with the girls wondering what the ships were doing.

On the first Sunday morning in Church as I was leading the service I became conscious of some men's voices harmonising at the back of the congregation. The sailors Ralph had spoken about had turned up for the morning service. Afterwards we chatted with them and invited them to come to the Chaplain's flat for tea when they were off duty. I shall never forget the afternoon the sailors were coming to tea, because we had an unexpected and extremely heavy rainstorm. Consequently answering the door I suddenly found myself facing eight sailors all soaked to the skin. Without stopping to say anything I quickly rummaged through my suitcase, and then managed to provide enough shirts for each one of them to have a dry one. Before they left I then facetiously asked them to pose on the front steps, so I could get a photo, each man with one of my shirts on - I wish I still had a copy to prove it!

One evening during the week a formidable Irish lady, married to a Spaniard, gave us some free tickets for an open-air ice show in the city's old bullring. Before the show she invited us to supper and the first thing on the menu was cold fish soup. I was seated opposite a Cuban Naval Officer who had jumped ship and hoped for political asylum in Spain. I don't normally drink alcohol, but as we tried to sip the soup it was so awful it made us want to vomit (we later learned it was made from the liquid in which mackerel had been cooked, and was therefore extremely oily!) Fortunately we saw a bottle of red wine so the pair of us managed to get the soup down by drinking large mouthfuls of wine in between small sips of soup. Despite this I must say however it was a great ice show that night, during which we were able to gaze up at the star-studded sky during the performance.

On the second Sunday, having got to know the sailors, we decided to have an informal meeting after the evening service. One of them (a North American Indian) had previously been a drug addict, and spoke of how this had almost destroyed his marriage and family. But how the Lord had powerfully changed him and remade his marriage - by which time most of us were in tears. He continued to write to us for several years afterwards. We were also invited to a meal on the aircraft carrier and were very impressed as both officers and other ranks all ate together. There was also an unlimited supply of American ice cream available from a machine where you helped yourself. You can imagine Deborah and Elizabeth were very impressed.

During the last few days I visited several Church members in hospital. Deputising for the Chaplain sometimes meant visiting English people on holiday that were ill. One afternoon I went to a large modern hospital called "El Hospital de los Principes de España". Up on the eleventh floor I visited a man who had been hit by a motorbike whilst on holiday and had the whole of his leg in plaster. He had been forced to stay behind after all his family had returned to England. A Spanish patient in his small ward had been trying to encourage him, but was unable to speak English. I thanked the Spanish patient and was then able to translate for him, and pray for them both.

Towards the end of the last week the American sailors invited us to go with them to watch a firework display at Franco's palace. It was of course late at night and was very impressive as we watched the fireworks and the floodlit fountains. Two of the sailors were married and I'm sure were missing their children as they lifted Deborah and Elizabeth up onto their shoulders.

On the last Sunday we were invited to lunch with the English Consul and his wife. We had known Derek and Grace Fernyhough in Santiago, in Chile, where he had been on the Embassy staff. One of the most memorable members of St George's was Mr Witty, a gentleman in his seventies, and one of the Churchwardens. He was very good with children and was often showing tricks to Deborah and Elizabeth. His son owned a very successful sports business in Barcelona. One day they took us on an outing into the country to their small farm, insisting on filling up our tank with petrol as we followed them. Our stay in Barcelona had been a wonderful experience and everyone had been so kind and generous.

We drove back to Lyon to put our car on the train in France again. After getting something to eat I asked Ann and the girls to get on board and I would follow. Our car had broken down twice during our stay so I wanted to see it safely on board. Of course it wouldn't start so I offered to drive it onto the train. Unfortunately because of this I was delayed getting on. However fortunately I did manage to scramble on right at the end, as the very long train was moving off. Walking down the extremely lengthy corridor I had to go virtually the whole length of the train. Finally arriving at our carriage I found Elizabeth in tears, she was convinced that "Daddy has been left behind!"

Possible Pastorates

Within my first three years I had a letter from Bishop Arturo Sanchez, head of the Anglican Diocese of Spain. He must have been notified through the SAMS that we had been missionaries in Chile and were now resident back in the U.K. Our chief qualification was that he knew we had a good command of Spanish and he wanted me to come to work in Madrid. In some ways this seemed attractive to me, considering all the aggro I was getting from the Parish hierarchy. However talking to Deborah and Elizabeth they had serious doubts and said "What would happen to

Grandma, we shall probably all finish up crammed in a flat some five storeys up with no garden?" My Mother was now living around the corner, as we had brought her up from London when she was eighty to be near to us. To take Grandma to Spain was just not practical or realistic as she was now eighty-three. The girls also told me they wanted to finish their studies as I think Deborah was at Basford Hall, and Elizabeth wanted to go there later. So I wrote to thank the Bishop for his invitation saying I really couldn't come. Initially I had thought to stay in the Parish for probably about seven years and then move on. I felt that would be a reasonable amount of time and then I would be ready to make a change. However looking back the Lord obviously had other plans.

The second job offer came later in 1988. This time I had a phone call from the Chairman of trustees of two Churches in Benidorm. There seemed to be some urgency and he appealed "Would you go out to see the present Pastor and consider the post?" This time it was just before Deborah got married so Ann said she was too busy to come with me. Anyway she didn't seem very keen on the idea. I would have two Churches, one Spanish speaking, and the other English. The latter congregation consisted of oil-rig workers from Norway and Sweden who preferred services in English.

I think I arranged a flight from Gatwick, and when I arrived there found the flight went at about 3.00am. I was fearful that if I booked a room I would oversleep so decided to bed down in the airport lounge. After a while I couldn't sleep so decided to find the chapel. It was empty with chairs around three sides. I sat there quietly praying asking the Lord to give me wisdom regarding the job offer. I really wasn't sure what I felt, and I don't think I had really discussed this much with my family. I needed the Lord's guidance. As I was sitting there with my eyes shut I sensed someone come and sit beside me. Opening my eyes he introduced himself as a retired American Naval Officer now working as a Pastor. He also wanted the Lord's guidance for his future and asked me to anoint him with oil. I wasn't sure how he expected me to do this, so I suggested he anoint me first and I would do the same for him afterwards. He was obviously prepared because he then produced a small bottle from his pocket and did the stuff. When it was my turn I was very nervous and consequently I poured too much oil over his head. He was as bald as an egg and to my alarm the oil ran all over his head. A bit like the oil running down Aaron's beard! (Psalm 133 v2). However he didn't seem too offended so we chatted briefly afterwards and then went our separate ways.

Arriving at Alicante airport I took a bus to stay for the week with a lovely English couple called Chris and Kathie Van Stratten. They were teachers who generously allocated me their small daughter Joy's bedroom. Their flat was far from ideal as they were living some eleven storeys up. Early every morning I telephoned the Church Office hoping to arrange an interview for the new job, but there was never any answer. Sometimes waiting at the bus stop opposite the flat I would watch Kathie, as she precariously hung out her washing over the balcony. During each day I tried to occupy myself by walking around all the time, and going back to their flat for supper. It was May and was raining miserably most days, so at lunchtime I usually bought a cup of coffee and sandwich out. As each day passed I got more fed up as it all seemed an absolute waste of time. Eventually I took a bus to Benidorm to see if I could find the Church. Finding a couple of friendly policemen I asked them if they knew of an English speaking Church, or possibly the Salvation Army, whom I presumed worked in Spain? But they couldn't help so I returned to my hosts flat again. Friday came and I rang the Church Office for the last time. To my surprise the secretary actually answered and said that the Pastor had been on holiday and had been showing some visitors around most of the week. Sitting on the plane on the return flight I continued to reflect and pray a bit. It seemed that maybe the Lord didn't want me to take the pastorate in Benidorm. He had answered my prayers and the answer was no!

The third possible pastorate came some time later when a letter from Chile arrived from the trustees of a Church in Viña del Mar - in fact very near to the Church where I had been ordained. This was an English speaking Church who needed a new minister. I'm sure they assumed I was receiving a pension from the SAMS, for the stipend was fairly sparse, and I think Ann's fare would not be paid. This was really not very attractive or practical, so I wrote declining their invitation.

By this time we had been in the Parish eleven years, and the Lord had not allowed me to escape - as I have to say I had considered several times. I also remember asking Canon Harry Sutton if he could put anything my way. Then finally Bishop David Pytches rang one day. David had of course ordained me in Chile and has always been very supportive. "John there is an Anglican Church in Southhall who need a new Vicar. The members are from a number of different ethnic backgrounds - West Indians, Asians and other races. They are lovely people used to an informal lively form of worship. I thought of you because I'm sure you would get on well there." I was encouraged to be asked and thanked

David. But remember saying to him that I could not go as I had a job to finish where the Lord had placed me. I suppose I was feeling a bit like Nehemiah who had said "I am doing a great work, so that I cannot come down." (Nehemiah 6 v3). In some ways this had been the most attractive job I had been offered. But in all seriousness I felt God had called me to this Parish and I must complete the job in hand. On all of these occasions I had discussed the possibility with the Churchwardens, and each time they said "John if you feel it would be right to move we understand. We support you and leave the decision up to you." There was of course my family to be considered, for the girls wanted to finish at college before moving, and we had stayed in England to look after my mother. I also said to my daughters "Who wants a geriatric pastor, I mean I will be retiring in a few years!" So we were finally to stay for seventeen years!

Chapter 13
ANOTHER VISIT TO SPAIN

Because of our time in Chile, through summer camps and other contacts there, we made friends with Juan and Carolina Zamora. He was a very experienced and gifted Pastor and later felt the Lord calling him to work in Spain. In the beginning they found the Church so different to South America. I remember Carolina saying working with one of their congregations was like "trying to walk through wet concrete!" In some ways not too dissimilar to what we were experiencing. So during their time in Spain we stayed with them in Seville, and visited the Churches Juan was in charge of.

My other object at that time was to do some research during Holy Week on the Roman Catholic Church. I was actually studying to do my 'A' level in Spanish at West Notts College at the time, and had an assignment to complete. Later I went on to pass my exams, and became a member of the "Institute of Linguists" at Clarendon College in Nottingham.

The city of Seville has some of the most traditional Roman Catholic Churches in Spain, and during Holy Week the daily processions are very elaborate and impressive. Each day the area where we were staying was seething with hundreds of people filling the streets to watch. The procession was usually led by a brass band, and a contingent of men dressed in Roman soldiers uniforms with large white plumes on their helmets. They were followed by a very large platform supported by forty men underneath it. On top were full sized images of Jesus, Pontus Pilate and other officials. The procession moved very slowly, the soldiers marching to the solemn beat of a drum. Every fifty yards or so the procession stopped to give the men a chance to rest. The platform was followed by a large number of men dressed in while robes, and wearing black "Capotes", or tall pointed hoods, similar to those used by the Klu Klux Klan. The whole thing was very dramatic and a bit sinister; I was told the men wearing these hoods did so as to hide their identity. I was also surprised to be informed that very few of these men were devout Catholics, only taking part in this annual event to gain favour with the Church authorities and raise Church funds. Quite a number were local politicians or sports personalities hoping to gain popularity.

The wooden figures looked very realistic each covered in gold leaf, and dressed in beautiful biblical type clothing. The figures were finally taken back and lodged in one of the large Churches until the next year. The images didn't belong to the Church but the Church accommodated them to save offending local politicians and sports people. During the evenings after the processions people would enjoy themselves in the cafes and bars, staying until quite late into the night. One night (I think it was Saturday) a local drunk took one of the metal barriers, used to control the crowds, and began crashing it into the Church doors. Finally he took a beer bottle and hurled it through the

Seville - Holy Week procession

glass window in the Church porch. Carolina said he was well known in the area, and the following morning I helped her sweep up the broken glass before the children came for Sunday School.

During our time in Seville we attended the very traditional Anglican Church on the street called Relator. At the beginning of the morning service Juan Zamora announced that we were English visitors who had previously worked in South America. I suppose we should not have been surprised because with usual reserve (or should I say Anglican fashion) no one spoke to us. That is to say one gentleman in the porch did, and speaking in Spanish told me he found all the ladies very beautiful! That rather amused me but then he explained he had been Church Treasurer for many years and was now totally blind! However in the evening we were invited to a Church Plant, where I preached in a much more friendly and informal service. This was held in some hired premises and attended by a number of young families with children. Then on the Monday, being a bank holiday, we were taken out for a Church outing and picnic. After our time with the Zamora family, we spent a few days in another friend's holiday apartment on the coast before returning home.

Chapter 14
GRAVE PROBLEMS

A Large Churchyard and Lots of Funerals

I shall never forget that within a few days of my arrival in the Parish I didn't know what had hit me because I had eight funerals in just over a week. Most of which were interments in the Churchyard. The first problem I encountered was that some families wanted a grave dug in a place of their own choice. I assured them that I would try to place the new grave near a relative's. But often where this was not practical I would have to take the next plot available. This was more orderly and practical from a maintenance point of view. Some time later after consultation we decided to dig double depth graves to conserve ground as we were using it up at quite a rate.

One weekend we had been away and on return I was astonished to find one of the local undertakers had dug a grave in the pathway. On appealing to him to take the next plot available he replied "Oh it's too late now, that would cause distress to the family." I now had a serious problem with the undertaker, and decided I needed to be firm and replied "All right if you refuse I will fill it in myself and you can dig another one in the proper place." So shovel in hand I filled in the grave in the pathway, and he was forced to dig another grave. As I was doing this Eric came over to dissuade me but I'd almost finished by then. Another day – in fact on Boxing Day morning – the phone rang somewhere after 7.00am - whilst I was still in bed. We were having a day off after all the Christmas services. It was the same undertaker "Vicar can you show me where I should dig the next grave I have a funeral!" "What's the urgency?" I enquired. "Oh I need to get things forward" he responded. I was astounded and annoyed, so pulling my clothes on over my pyjamas I was forced to get over to the Churchyard.

Later we had a more congenial relationship and I remember going down to his premises. He asked me to call because he wanted to show me his new chapel of rest. Arriving at his house his wife offered me a cup of tea, and I was fascinated to see a new coffin on the kitchen table. He explained that this was because the weather was so cold that the French polish would not dry. It needed a warm temperature otherwise the polish would remain cloudy. Later he asked me if he might put some beehives in our garden. I decided against this as it might compromise my position.

Regarding headstones Southwell Diocese had quite strict regulations about the size, shape, style, stone and the type of memorial. For example white marble was not permitted, and only certain colours of granite were allowed. The Parish was on the boundary with Derby Diocese so they had their own regulations, which were often quite different. This caused confusion for both the monumental masons and the bereaved families. The bereaved relatives sometimes accusing me of "being heartless and insensitive", when I had to explain the design of the memorial did not comply with the regulations.

I also remember two specific occasions when the stonemasons placed headstones on the wrong graves. This was because they were in too much of a hurry to confirm with Eric, or myself, the location of the graves. One day an irate man complained that he had been grieving over the wrong grave, which he thought was his wife's. I explained that this was not my fault; he however demanded an apology. So I wrote a carefully worded letter saying how sorry I was that he had been so distressed. Ironically, to my surprise, someone told me later he had not even been living with his wife for eight years. He was in fact living with another woman. The other situation was worse when a widow had been placing flowers on what she thought was her husband's grave. We of course had to explain that in fact it was not her husband's grave. Again the masons had placed the memorial on the wrong one. She was so extremely distressed that we all tried to console her but this was to no avail.

This time the new Churchwardens eventually came up with an idea. All would meet one evening, dig down to the coffin, and take off the brass plate with the deceased's name on. Then replacing all the earth would place the plate just below ground level to show to her that this really was her husband's grave. For me this was a very stressful situation, and I was extremely grateful for the Churchwardens support. So that evening after supper I put on my old working clothes and boots. Finding I had time to spare I went upstairs but unfortunately nodded off. Around 8.30pm I awoke to hear voices downstairs in the kitchen. Quickly going down I found the group all talking to Ann and drinking coffee. "What happened to you?" they exclaimed. To be truthful I'm not sure exactly what I said but I was extremely embarrassed! Fortunately I think the lady was finally convinced but it was a predicament I cannot forget. However, praise the Lord the problem was resolved.

Churchyard Maintenance

The Churchyard had been enlarged and the oldest part (around the Church) had been buried over twice. My predecessor had spent many long hours each week mowing with an enormous old ride-on motor mower. As much as I tried somehow I couldn't get the hang of this. I was scared because it tended to dig into the ground, stall and then throw me off! In addition to the previous Vicar's ceaseless work one of the Churchwardens also used to spend a large amount of time cutting the grass. Yet the task was so enormous the problem was never going to be satisfactorily resolved.

I recall one afternoon two elderly ladies calling at the Vicarage. They were distressed to find the family grave overgrown with weeds and long grass, so they asked "Could the grave be tidied up please?" They had come from Nottingham and couldn't get over very often. I sympathised fully but explained we had no staff to deal with the problem. So I eventually said "Well I was just about to go visiting two people in hospital. Do you think I should postpone that and go over and tend the grave?" Shaking their heads they replied "Oh no you should make the visiting your priority!" Later I was greatly relieved when I was able to notify them that a man down the lane would tend the grave regularly for a small sum, and the two ladies were so grateful. Sadly however many of the graves were left completely unattended and overgrown. Although I remember around Easter children would sometimes come and take daffodils growing in the Churchyard and place them on graves that had no flowers. One morning I had a difficult exchange with a gravedigger, although we had a notice that requested no dogs, he insisted on bringing his dog with him, and kept a mobile radio playing loudly whilst working. I complained about this explaining that people's dogs were fouling the graves. But he responded by saying "If you don't like the way I do things perhaps you're in the wrong job!" I quickly decided to slip away and get on with other things, but a thought kept going through my mind "I'm a Pastor not a cemetery superintendent why should I have to deal with this sort of thing?"

Closure Order

Some time later I received a telephone call from a high official in London. She was ringing to say that my predecessor had applied for a closure order and this had been granted. But to my disappointment it turned out that this only applied to the area immediately around the Church. Somehow a local paper got hold of this and wanted to know why I hadn't applied for a closure order before! Of course in theory I could now oblige the local council to maintain that part, and they rather reluctantly accepted the task.

Yet sadly in the future the grass was never cut regularly, and I had to frequently ring up to remind them. In fact when my daughter Deborah was married photos show the grass was very long and untidy. Although to my astonishment at some point they did provide a hundred new rose-bushes.

Later an unwelcome surprise came with the advent of wheelie bins. Suddenly the local council insisted that the Church should pay for the removal of refuse, such as wreaths, wrappings and dead flowers. Baffled and annoyed I told them that almost all this stuff came from the local community, and had very little to do with those who attended Church. Next when wheelie bins came in they even expected the Church to buy them, treating us in the same way as a business! Fortunately they finally climbed down and I was much relieved, for previously they had been emptying six to eight dustbins every week.

I'm sorry to bore you with all this depressing detail but feel I need to mention these things so that people can get a better understanding of the feeling of frustration that Parish clergy often have to cope with! Of course I must also say that all this business about Churchyards was new and utterly beyond me. When I had been pastor of two different Churches in Chile neither had a Churchyard. Although in the cities there were usually fairly large old established city cemeteries. Whilst working as a Hospital Chaplain in Chile the custom there was that most people went to the local Catholic Church for funerals. Later, serving as a curate in Harrow the Churchyard at Christ Church had a closure order. So all the burials I had previously officiated at had always been in local authority cemeteries. Eddie was very lucky as his Church at Roxeth, South Harrow already had a closure order when he came. Today from my experience as Incumbent I feel extremely strongly that local authorities should maintain all Churchyards. And what's more they should also be responsible for the regulations for the memorials and headstones. After all they are getting a local cemetery on the cheap! Taking over the Churchyards would save a lot of confusion and considerably lessen the heartache and stress caused to so many bereaved families. This done, clergy could then concentrate on the task they were called and trained to do, namely preaching the Gospel and carrying out the pastoral care of the people in their Parishes!

To be fair though, in addition to the hundred new rose bushes the Council did provide, they later asked if they could reduce the size of the rose beds. Following a time and work study they had made, it showed it would make mowing much easier and reduce the time involved. Yet the weeding of the rose beds was still neglected. So, as we longed and prayed for an answer, we began thinking about the new people now attending Church - perhaps some of these families might like to consider adopting a rose bed. David Lester, one of our Churchwardens, did a good job enlisting about six of the new families now attending Church to adopt a flowerbed and look after it. Robert Murray and Eric Papworth took on the job of mowing, and I would also try to do my bit as well.

There is a story told that early one morning some of the new dads were standing just inside Church by the hymnbook table before the service. An older Church member in her seventies also arrived early. Assuming the problem of weeding the rose beds was uppermost in people's mind she said "Oh I would like to do a sponsored strip!" Of course she didn't realize what she had actually said. But the young dads looked at each other and just didn't know where to put their faces. I must say that this was before the "Calendar Girls" had been heard of. The dads had to try so hard to contain their laughter. I mean it doesn't take much imagination to conjure up a picture of a very committed Church member in her late seventies, doing a 'strip tease' to support the Church! Yet as far as I know this incident has never been spoken of since.

Chapter 15
BROTHERS TOGETHER AND ENCOURAGEMENT

The Blessing of Brothers in Unity (Psalm 133)

One great oasis for me at the beginning of my time in the Parish was a meeting of the local ministers. This was not a formal thing and I don't remember how it came about. We met mostly at the Vicarage and the group consisted of a number of ministers from different denominations, almost all from the Parish.

At first there was myself, David Grieve, (my then Curate), Geoffrey Harris one of the Methodist ministers, Scott Schade from the Church of Christ, and Guy Fouts who was Rector of Pinxton. Later Paul Williamson also joined us, when he was at St Mary's, Westwood. I'm sure one reason for coming together was because we all wanted to see a degree of renewal in our congregations. In our Churches there seemed to be a fear of any form of change and this often resulted in stubborn opposition. One minister's organist was resigning because the new minister wanted to include some new songs he had chosen for the anniversary. Our congregations were throwing all sorts of spanners in the works. At one stage several of us went to a John Wimber conference, when one of the ministers said to me "John if my Church knew I was attending a charismatic conference I would get the sack!" Later when Billy Graham was coming to Sheffield most of us went to the preparation meetings there for ministers. I was thrilled because this campaign was going to be such a fantastic opportunity for preaching the Gospel, yet we experienced so much stubborn indifference from some of our Churches.

In this context our ministers' meetings were so refreshing and helpful because it gave all of us a chance to share experiences and problems, and pray for each other in confidence. The wife of one minister was suffering from severe stress, and he had financial problems. Things he really didn't want to discuss with anyone. So at times we would listen to him pour all this out for an hour or more. Our meetings together could be so therapeutic, although often all we did was lend a sympathetic ear. A very important thing I found so interesting was most of us had worked in Churches in other countries which gave us a wider view of the Church that was not so hampered by our traditions.

Nominated as Council Member

In 1982 I had a phone call from the then General Secretary of the South American Mission Society. Canon Philip King (whom I had worked under) said "We have been thinking and would like to nominate you to become a member of the Society's General Council, if you are prepared to stand?" I decided I should discuss this with my Curate David Grieve, as it would mean attending three residential conferences a year, usually of two or three day duration. These were always during the week, so I would not be absent at weekends.

David responded very positively saying "John it seems a great idea to me because it's always good to find out what the Lord is doing in different parts of His kingdom." So I was elected a member of the General Council and served for the next ten years. I eventually stood down by which time I felt it was important to be replaced by a younger person. However by then Bishop Bill Flagg had succeeded Philip King. Bill rang me to say how disappointed he was to hear I was standing down and to ask me to reconsider my decision. I had of course known Bill for over 30 years, for he had worked in Chile before us, and had served as Diocesan Bishop in a number of countries in South America. I thanked him saying it was such an encouragement to know I was still wanted and appreciated. Nevertheless I was still convinced I should stand down saying "Some younger blood was needed on the Council."

Conferences and Conversions

The diocese usually had an annual conference at Swanwick. I can't remember much about those now, except that when the bar opened you couldn't see for smoke. Although the meals, cake, coffee and homemade scones and jam were fabulous. The thing that really astounded me happened on the afternoon Stuart Blanch, former Archbishop of York, gave some excellent addresses on Matthew's gospel. That afternoon as I looked around the auditorium I could see six clerics sound asleep!

However at one of the renewal conferences at Swanwick we were told to go back to our Parishes and pray in our Churches. The suggestion was to move around from pew to pew, and pray in the seat where you knew the person who normally sat there. So I went home and spent over two hours on that Sunday afternoon after the conference praying in each person's seat. Incredibly, I can't remember exactly how, but afterwards the atmosphere in Church began to change considerably!

Then a very exciting thing happened another Sunday after one of these conferences. I felt the Lord was urging me to invite people to give their lives to Christ. So at the end of the Family Service I made an appeal. I was so surprised, and absolutely overjoyed, for two men in the congregation stood up. One was Arthur and the other Martin. Arthur who was in his seventies had been greatly influenced by the gracious witness of Annie Jacques, a lady in her late seventies, who had started working with Ann in the Sunday School.

The other was Martin, someone I had been warned about, because he was often involved in fights when he had been drinking. One Sunday evening he actually threatened to punch the Youth Fellowship's speaker on the nose. But this Sunday morning Martin confessed to me that he had come into Church full of hatred for everyone. Yet instead of encountering hatred in return he was overwhelmed by the love he found amongst us.

Chapter 16
VERGER APPOINTED

As I remarked earlier on my first visit, whilst walking around the Churchyard, someone spoke to me who later turned out to be the gravedigger. Later I found Eric to be an absolute mine of information. In addition to the Church burial registers he had his own small book containing the details of hundreds of graves. He was now well into his seventies, and had taken up grave digging since retiring from the pit. Both Eric and his wife Lucy were very dedicated members of the Church. I was, by the way, the first Vicar Church people had spoken to by his Christian name. On the other hand I found it quite unacceptable that some older members insisted on addressing Eric by his surname. However from the beginning Eric and I were always on Christian name terms.

Eric was such a help. When there was a funeral I often needed someone to put the heating on, and hand out hymnbooks and generally welcome people. At other times people asked about the whereabouts of a certain grave. Even after going through the burial registers you could spend hours searching for a grave. I specifically remember one afternoon when there was about three inches of snow on the ground. Eric and I had to spend almost three hours trying to find a grave in the Churchyard, following the request of a young relative from Mansfield. The trouble was so many people just assumed that the Vicar should know exactly where every grave was!

I would interject here that later Nora Langton, our very faithful and industrious Church Secretary, very kindly agreed to deal with the enormous amount of mail I received with inquiries about family graves. Many of these came from overseas, from Australia, New Zealand, Canada and the States. These enquiries were often very involved and time consuming.

I had inherited a system where some Churches still employed their own gravedigger and this was a task Eric had done so faithfully for a long time. This meant often in the winter, in all weathers, come rain, wind, sleet or snow, I would go over as Eric was digging a grave. He would nearly always be working wearing an old raincoat, with a sack around his shoulders, old trousers and mining boots. The thing that really worried me was that so often he was soaked to the skin, and for a man in his seventies this was unacceptable. Chatting to him one day I said "You know you remind me of my dad, and I certainly wouldn't allow my dad to dig graves at your age." Eric responded with a slight chortle, and then confessed that his daughters had already asked him to retire. So I asked him to consider that what I most needed was a Verger "Would he please take on the job?" To my delight Eric agreed.

Later when I raised the subject I was astounded when one senior member of the Church Council objected very strongly! "Why what's your reason?" I challenged him, and his answer was bordering on an insult. The answer was "Well he's so scruffy, wearing those old boots and trousers, and when people see him what will they think of our Church?" I was hurt and so angry at the response. It showed no appreciation for all that Eric had been doing, plus a complete disregard for his welfare! So controlling my frustration I said "O.K. but if I ask him not to wear his working clothes, and put on a cassock and polish his shoes I can't see what's your objection!" So praise the Lord Eric was appointed as Verger. In fact he and his wife Lucy continued to clean the Church. Eric no longer dug graves, but continued to cut the grass and tidy up, and the funeral directors were then responsible for employing gravediggers. Previously I had been fed up with the way the gravediggers had haggled over their rates of pay when I approached them. So from that time onwards this issue was for the undertakers to sort out.

No Smoke without Fire

Each year at the end of the summer the grass was knee high in the older part of the Churchyard. Eric would therefore carry out a controlled fire to burn off the long grass, as it would always grow up again in the spring. It was an impossible task to cut such a large area of grass. One day a lady complained saying that the smoke was making her washing dirty. On another occasion Fred Crawford, one of the Churchwardens, was working with Eric. All at once to my great surprise a fire appliance had drawn up outside the Church. A niggardly neighbour had called the fire brigade! Just before the Fire Officer walked into the Churchyard the lady's husband began haranguing Eric, and in the confusion stamped on Fred's foot. This time the complaint was that the smoke was blowing into the couple's bedroom windows, but as Fred pointed out, the wind was actually blowing in the opposite direction. In the end the Fire Officer said "Don't worry in the future just give us a ring beforehand - we shan't trouble coming out again." Yet I felt there was never going to be an end to the complaints about the Churchyard. On another occasion a person complained to Eric as he was burning off the long grass. To my great amusement Eric then came up with the classic remark "Well lady what do you expect me to do eat it?"

I would really like to mention just one incident that demonstrated Eric's great support and concern for me. A resident had died at St Helen's Court, the sheltered flats on Lindley Street. The old lady had no relatives living in the area but had a brother living down in Kent. He had suffered for many years with mental illness and could be very unpredictable. A couple of days before the funeral I was told that the brother was coming to Church. The service went off well and I had forgotten all about him.

Then just before I left Church the man came up to me and wanted to know why his sister had died, and why no one had told him she was ill. I really had no idea and had to say so. Immediately he began to get very aggressive and followed me into the vestry and slammed the door! At once I realized I was at risk but couldn't get out as he was blocking my way. I soon ran out of things to say, was getting worried, and wanted to get off home. I had no idea what to do then I heard a voice "Are you all right John?" It was Eric, now the Verger, whom I thought had gone home. I can't remember what I said, but fortunately Eric had a key and quickly opened the vestry door. At that the man immediately pushed past us and rushed off. Eric had been waiting for me being concerned for my safety had not gone home until he knew everything was O.K.

Chapter 17
BRIDES AND WEDDINGS

Having spoken about burials, another of what we call "the occasional offices" concerns brides. I asked my family what they remember of Vicarage life? Deborah said "Well every Thursday evening we had to sit in the dining room because you interviewed wedding couples in our lounge." One of my sons said "Well we have to realise that our house was really your business premises!" The problem was that the study was too small, and the Church too cold. Over the years I must have conducted at least four hundred weddings during my time in the Parish. Ladies still come up to me occasionally today and say "Mr Jacklin you married me thirty years ago." Of course I have to confess sometimes I don't actually remember who they are. But many of the weddings were such happy occasions, especially at the times when Ann and I were invited to the reception. Of course we couldn't always accept them when there were as many as three weddings on the same afternoon. I used to include a suitable short address as part of the service. These were usually well received, and one guest came to thank me afterwards saying "I've never heard anyone speak that way about the twenty-third psalm before." Another day during the address some of the congregation seemed particularly disinterested and were chatting during the service. I was a bit miffed by this, and then I noticed one person pointing across the Church towards the organ. What was fascinating them was a small mouse perched on top of the organ console. It was just sitting up on his haunches and washing with its front paws, oblivious to his audience.

I would briefly like to say that weddings in South America are quite different to the U.K. Let me just mention the wedding of my own goddaughter whose dad had been my Bishop. Discovering we would be returning to Chile for a few weeks Margaret asked me to give her away. Church marriages are

Wedding of Rev Enrique Lago & Margaret, my goddaughter (Chile)

not legally recognised in Chile, so everyone has to go to the Civil Registry Office. Christians obviously want a Church service, so this happens afterwards. So Margaret and Enrique did the legal bit first, three days before. This consisted of a small number of close family, plus witnesses, going to sign the registers. A few days later we had a fantastic wedding service on a Friday evening in Church. I gave the bride away, and her dad presided at the service.

It was a warm summer evening, so afterwards the reception was held in the Church grounds under the stars, going on late into the night. I have to confess I think this pattern is better than the English one. Firstly of course the couple have to prove to the Registrar that they don't have a spouse somewhere else. Regarding the issue of divorce this doesn't seem to be a problem in England now. During my time I did however conduct several services of blessing after a civil ceremony. But I never wanted to get involved in all the nitty-gritty of why people had been divorced, (except perhaps of practising Christians). I also feel, as with baptisms, if people are not Christians why come into Church? There are some very attractive venues today in hotels and country houses, with a minister in attendance. Weddings in Church mean couples have to make vows before God, when many people today don't even believe in Him. I was once told at a clergy chapter meeting in Harrow that the Church in this country has only been marrying people for a little over a thousand years. So before that we presumably only had some sort of civil ceremony in England.

Wedding of my daughter Elizabeth
with Eric Papworth

Chapter 18
A HEALING MINISTRY

"They shall place their hands on sick people."

I have seen so many people healed over the years, many of course in Chile, but also a number in the U.K. I have continued to go to seminars and conferences on healing when I could. More recently I discovered our local Newsagent, who is a Sikh, needed a heart operation. The family were very worried so once in hospital I asked the son how his dad was? He answered they would have to operate but weren't sure if it would be successful. I offered to pray for his father and went to see him in the City Hospital. As I sat at the bedside suddenly the whole family arrived and gathered around, the men in their turbans and the ladies in their saris. I have never before prayed in a situation like that, but I decided as we had talked about it beforehand I should go ahead. After praying I slipped away leaving the family around the bed. Two days later the son rang to say his father was much improved, and soon came home and has continued to be well. Again since retirement, I noticed a Muslim lady in pain in the waiting room in Derby Royal Infirmary. She told me she was waiting for the results of tests and was obviously worried. I didn't say anything then but began praying for her for a period of some weeks until she started to look better. Finally I mentioned I had been praying for her over several weeks. She graciously smiled and thanked me.

I remember a John Wimber conference in Harrogate where he announced that there were five women with cancer in the auditorium that the Lord wanted to heal. Wimber asked them to stand up but no one responded. He was obviously a bit puzzled by this but affirmed the Lord had told him this, and the evening meeting finished. I think he also remarked that the Lord was making him wait to humble him. The next morning, before the session started, it was announced that since the previous evening's meeting the five women had come forward to say they had all been healed. I feel that I must interject here to say that I have of course also seen people who have received prayer for healing who have not been healed.

In my first year in the Parish I was excited and encouraged by the first instance of healing. A Church member's elderly mother was taken into hospital with serious breathing difficulties. I visited her on the third day she had been hospitalised. Most of the family were gathered around the bed when I arrived all looking very worried. Suddenly the old lady became very agitated and snatched her mask off. A member of the family quickly went to find a nurse and the minutes ticked by. None appeared and I felt I needed to take some action. Remembering what Jesus had done I asked the family to leave me alone with their mother. Then taking both of her hands in mine I said "Look Jesus loves you very much and wants to give you His peace and healing. Please put the mask back on." To my surprise she complied, I prayed for her, and within a few minutes she had regained her composure. A few days later she returned home completely well, and was soon getting on with the cooking and looking after the family once more. She continued to get on fine and lived for another three years much to everyone's astonishment and delight.

One day I received a phone call to say that Adam, Mary's small son, was seriously ill. I would like to include her account. Here I would like to quote Mary's own words. "Adam was prone to bronchitis and so made regular trips to the doctors, and we got used to it. But on this occasion the first antibiotics did not seem to do any good. So the doctor tried another but things did not improve. On Monday night we had a really bad night. Adam was having nightmares about spiders and other things coming out of the walls. In the morning I phoned the doctor who said he thought Adam had pneumonia. We had to get him to hospital straight away. When someone is ill two days is like a lifetime, especially when they do not respond to treatment. Adam wasn't responding by Thursday so they told me they had to send away for another antibiotic. It should arrive by Friday teatime. Stewart and I took it in turns to watch over Adam. By Thursday night we were both convinced he was not going to make it. We came out of the hospital sat in the car and cried. Instead of going home we went to see John and Ann who prayed and read the Bible with us and eventually we went home. We didn't expect to get any sleep, but found we both slept all night. Stewart had to go into work the next day and so I went to the hospital by myself. Soon after I arrived Adam sat up quite well demanding "Ready Brek" which the hospital did not have. When the nurse mentioned the antibiotics would soon be here I had to say but he doesn't need them, for I knew in my heart the Lord had healed him. What we did not know was that while we slept John and Ann had spent time praying into the early hours."

I remember visiting Adam each day at the hospital. He was too ill to say much, so the Lord gave me the idea of taking a small metal figure on a swing to place on his locker. If you pushed the figure it went backwards and forwards for ages - "perpetual motion". I did of course pray with Adam each day. We were absolutely astounded and so joyful at Adam's healing, praising the Lord for what He had done! And we have continued a great friendship with Mary and Stewart ever since.

One year we were coming up to the AGM and one of the young dads had been wonderfully converted through a Salvation Army colleague at work. Brian was overjoyed in his new relationship with Jesus. Indeed coming home from work he would wind the car window down so that others could hear tapes of Christian songs and music. He was nominated to stand for the Church Council and we were all looking forward to him being elected. Then the blow fell - suddenly this 33 year old was diagnosed with cancer. So with his wife's permission I took seventeen Church members to pray at their home. By then sadly Brian was already too weak to stand and stayed upstairs in bed. I had spent time that afternoon praying with him and he said to me he had been reading the 23rd Psalm. "I believe the Lord's my shepherd and I'm sure God is going to heal me." The seventeen of us met that evening downstairs with the local Pentecostal Pastor from Jacksdale. We spent some time praying together for Brian's healing. At the end of the evening I asked Pastor Spearing what he felt was going to happen. He replied that within 48 hours we would know. It was therefore to our enormous sorrow and sadness that Brian died two days later and everyone was devastated. The Church was packed for the funeral and I shall never forget the group of young dads all standing at the back around the font overwhelmed with tears. We had prayed and prayed, and Brian had believed, but he had not been healed. We took many months to get over Brian's death and it seemed it would set us back for a very long time.

Later I reflected on what John Wimber had said. When his Church began to pray for healing many people died. Yet after a year people did begin to be healed. Wimber said his Church later became like a hospital with different people coming in for healing each week, and surely this was what Jesus would have wanted. The healing ministry happens in so many Churches today. Like South American Christians, and others in so many parts of the world, they actually believe the command and promise Jesus gave His disciples to "place their hands on sick people, and they will get well." (Matthew 10 v8; Mark 16 v18). Speaking to Jehovah Witnesses this seems to be something they completely overlook.

One year at the end of summer a young teacher started coming to the Parish Church. She had only been a Christian for a short time and had just been confirmed in Sheffield before moving into our village. However within a few months I was informed that she had suffered a series of serious throat infections. In the end she was finally diagnosed with cancer of the throat.

As I had been visiting her she agreed to allow us to pray and lay hands on her for healing. So a group of us went to her house to pray several times. The husband, also a teacher, was very sceptical and I discovered he was an atheist. But praise God over a period of some weeks she began to get better and was finally healed.

There was also a Church member's mother who was ill with bad headaches so the daughter asked if we could pray for her. Protocol demanded that I ask permission from her Incumbent as she lived in another Parish. He agreed to us taking a group to go to the house to pray and lay hands on her mother. To my delight he actually asked if he could accompany us saying "Could I come with you because this is not part of our Church tradition and I've never seen this done before." We went two or three times and there was some improvement but she was not completely healed.

One day a very faithful member of the Church went into hospital for an operation. She was a single lady probably about sixty and had very few relatives so I visited her several times. She was not getting better and one problem was that she was refusing to eat. One lunchtime the Ward Sister said to me "Do you think you could come each day and help feed her, she seems to respond to you." Realising she wouldn't eat the hospital food each day I would buy some on the way to the hospital. One of our Link Missionaries, home on leave from Africa also came with me. She was well known to Ivy as they had taught in the same school. Even trying to feed Ivy with some yoghurt was literary impossible - she just allowed the stuff to run out of the corner of her mouth. In the end Annette looked into Ivy's face and said "Look the Lord loves you very much and wants you to get better, please eat the food we've brought." Then placing her hands on the patient she began to pray. During the days that followed Ivy gradually began to improve. Finally the Ward Sister said to me "Look, I'm an atheist and don't like clergymen. You know Ivy is a manic depressive, but I have to say your treatment is working!" Ivy returned home and was confined to bed for several weeks. She still had a drainage tube in, as the wound continued suppurating, so Stephanie and Fran and other young mums changed the bed linen each day. They even took the sheets home to wash, until the District Nurse arranged a daily delivery of clean linen. Members of the Youth Fellowship also came to move furniture, and get a bed down from upstairs, and they even cut the front hedge. So the healing process was a real team effort. I have never believed I had the gift of healing but have just carried out Jesus' commission to His disciples (Mark 16 v18;

Luke 10 v.9). I always like to get others to lay on hands with me, and pray with me in obedience to Jesus' command.

I Believe in the Resurrection

One year a group of us, including Ernie Hill, Paul Knight and Norman Ramsden, went to a Bill Subritsky conference in Brighton called "The Battle Belongs to the Lord". We were very fortunate as some kind Christian friends in Preston Park provided us with hospitality. My purpose for our group was to receive some teaching on healing and the ministry of the Holy Spirit. I asked the Church Council to pay Ernie and Paul's fees as part of their ongoing training. We arrived in Brighton early to enable us to find parking, and having plenty of time went to get some coffee. Being a Christian conference we looked around and decided to join a small group of people at their table. I introduced our group and asked them where they were from. They said they were from a small Church in Poole that had not been going very long. "How did your Church start then?" I asked. The incredible answer came "We raised someone from the dead!" There was then a stunned silence! Eventually plucking up courage I asked "Please tell us about it?" "Well about five of us used to meet for prayer on Sunday afternoons" one answered. "One afternoon we were at prayer when we had a phone call. A lady rang to say her husband had just died and would we come and pray for him please. We looked at each other, wondering how to respond, and finally decided we must to do something. We had never had a request like this before, but eventually decided we must go to the house. We were ushered upstairs where the gentleman was in bed, and then kneeling around the bed we began to pray. We had never prayed for a dead person before but felt at least we ought to pray to comfort the widow. We must have prayed anything from three quarters of an hour or more. Suddenly we couldn't believe it - for his eyelids flickered, his eyes opened and he sat up. We called his wife, and eventually we went home, promising to call back later in the week. Then on the Friday we heard that he had passed away again." What an astounding story! But I felt I must ask the men what they felt when the man died again? They replied that the wife had said her husband had not been a Christian before, but following the miracle he had given his life to Christ. She knew he had now gone to be with Jesus because the Lord had given him a second chance!

One afternoon at the conference we were waiting for the session to begin. Just before I suddenly developed a terrible headache. I wanted to leave the auditorium because I couldn't concentrate. However Paul realised this, and turned to me and said "Well you know what we ought to do!" So immediately placing his hands on me he began to pray. Before the session started the headache was considerably better.

Chapter 19
CARAVANS AND CURATES

Caravan Holidays for Clapped out Clergy

I feel here I would like to relate how David and Jane Grieve finally came to work with us. Through our friendship and working with Bishop Colin Bazley and his wife Barbara in Chile, we came to know Colin's sister. Whilst in Harrow we were not too far from Heathrow. So on one occasion we went to see Colin and Barbara off one Sunday evening, as they were on their way back to Chile after a short stay in England. Unfortunately Ann and I were delayed going to the airport by a heavy rainstorm. Arriving late at the departure lounge we saw a group of friends and supporters but then realised the plane had gone. How depressing! Talking to one couple the wife said to us "I am Colin's sister what a shame you missed them, why don't you come down to Devon and stay a few days on the farm with us sometime?" So thus began a series of wonderful times at "Spicery", and we developed a great friendship with Michael and Pauline. Over the years we enjoyed many family holidays on the farm, first camping and then later in a large old caravan we kept there. In conversation one day we told Pauline and Michael that the work in the Parish was hard going but we soon hoped to get a Curate. Unbeknown to us a few days later Pauline put an advert in a Christian magazine offering "Caravan holidays for Clapped out Clergy". Michael's father had been an Anglican clergyman and he knew that clergy often didn't take a holiday. Out of the blue one young couple that replied to the advert were David and Jane Grieve. During their stay at the farm Pauline explained that we were in dire need of a colleague to help with the young people's work. So it was to our great delight that David contacted me.

Curate Saga ends and Young Peoples work Commences

Following several conversations with the local authority they allotted us a council house for David and his family. At first they argued that he had to be resident in the area to qualify. I then explained that David and family were moving down from Liverpool to work with me.

I also added that he would be of considerable value from a social angle working with families on the estate. Again I received so much encouragement before David's arrival with Church members supporting me. Mary and her mother offered to redecorate the house. The mother papering the kitchen very expertly - something she was extremely good at. Mary had been one of the Sunday School teachers when we first arrived.

69

Later as I prayed about things I really felt that she should worship at her own Parish Church. Mary graciously agreed and the Lord confirmed this to her, so later she and Stuart became very effective working with the young people at Brinsley.

A short time after David and Jane Grieve came to the Parish they started a Pathfinder club with twenty-eight young teenagers meeting in their home after school. On Sundays the youngsters attended a Bible class in Church. This was in addition to the work in the Sunday school with the younger children under Ann and her

Rev David & Jane Grieve with Katie

helpers. The Curate's presence on the estate was also a great blessing to families who normally never came to Church.

It was a tremendous encouragement to me having David take his share with preaching and services. He was very good at that, and I especially valued his knowledge of the Canons when I was in difficulty. Until then I had been preaching twice most Sundays and even more some weeks. Peter, my son, still remembers when I was often in the study as late as 1.30am on Sunday morning preparing my sermons for the day. Of course sometimes the old guard would get David on his own and try to force a wedge between what I had said and his opinion. But they got nowhere because David and I stood together, and he was always so loyal.

For example we had just begun to get lay people to do the intercessions during the evening service. So when I was away one weekend someone complained to David "The Vicar should do the prayers!" "But the Vicar's not here" responded David, which rather nonplussed the objector. David and Jane were with us for about three years and then went to take their own Parish.

Chapter 20
EVANGELISM

Ridley Mission

One of the most valuable and lasting legacies David left us was his suggestion that we arrange a mission with students from Ridley Hall Cambridge. This was David's old college and in preparation a few of us went to down to the college to meet the students. The mission had to be booked about two years in advance. I think a team of twelve students came with Hugo de Waal, their Principal. Each of our house groups was expected to support two students in prayer and hospitality. At the beginning the biggest challenge was the hospitality - something the Church had never done before. The provision of an evening meal seemed to worry some members, but the Principal emphasised "We don't expect to be fed like kings - something simple will suffice." In the end Church members responded well and were extremely motherly. My Mother told me she took compassion on her student and actually mended a shirt for him as she felt it had seen better days. We discovered after that his father was actually a famous bishop!

Each morning the team met at the Vicarage led by the Principal for planning and prayer. Hugo de Waal spoke each evening in Church on a different theme, with students visiting the homes of Church members during the day. One person converted was Robert Murray who was visited by a student called Nick. One evening it was decided to visit the local pubs, and I was detailed to accompany them.

Turning up at the White Lion many people immediately wanted to buy me drinks. Although I don't drink, I did accept a half pint and made it last as long as possible.

Afterwards at the Horse and Jockey the students first went to the upper room where the young people gathered. A few minutes later coming downstairs the students became rather concerned when two young men began talking to me, behaving in a rather aggressive manner, almost pinning me to the wall. They need not have worried because these two characters were my sons Peter and Stephen putting on an act!

On the last Sunday the students planned the morning service. This included a sketch written by the students. They also wanted to divide the congregation into small groups for discussion. I disagreed with that saying it wouldn't work. But I was proved to be absolutely wrong because people just turned round and talked over the pews. I would really like to know the number of Church members who were converted at the time. However the lasting impact of the mission was immeasurable, and it became such a growth factor in the life of our Church.

Billy Graham comes to Sheffield

In 1984 Billy Graham was due to come to the U.K. for his last live campaign. I still remember his first campaign in the early 1950's in London, and the tremendous impact that made. Indeed many of those converted then later became ordained ministers in the Church of England. Robert Murray had already become a Christian during the Ridley Mission, so he was very keen about the Sheffield Mission.

The event was placed on the Church Council agenda, but to say there was very little interest is a great understatement. When first raised there was complete silence and indifference. Robert was however not to be put off and suggested we book a double-decker bus to take people there. "Who will go on the bus?" came the question. After a pointless discussion Robert said "Well I suggest we go ahead, and we can fill it up by inviting people from the village." Very bravely Nora Langton, our Church Secretary, supported the proposal so we booked the bus. Nora was always ready to help and advise. One evening the Pathfinder leaders had some youngsters playing games in the Churchyard. Suddenly an angry member of the Church came over and complained saying "This is sacred ground not a playground!" However Nora soon found some rules in the Churchwardens Handbook, and reassured me that as long as a member of the Church Council was present organised games were in order. At one stage I was getting so many requests, mainly from abroad in Australia, Canada, and the States, requesting details of their family graves or details in the Church registers. This involved an enormous amount of time, but once again Nora came to my aid. Having lived in the area all her life she knew so many of these families personally, and gallantly offered to deal with these enquiries in the future.

Returning to the Sheffield campaign the next task was to invite the people and this fell myself and to our next-door neighbour Mick, who had been long term unemployed. He was very gifted musically and had begun playing his violin in Church, as part of our newly formed music group. For the next week or two we went out house to house, knocking on doors. Normally going out late afternoon when it was hoped we could catch people home from work. People generally welcomed us courteously but a few didn't. One warm summer evening we called at a flat where the front window was open with the curtains billowing out in the breeze. The television was obviously on so we knew someone was at home. When a teenager came to the door we asked her if her dad was in please? We waited and after a considerable pause eventually a bleary eyed man in his vest came to the door. He was not at all pleased and demanded grumpily what we wanted, and when we told him he quickly dismissed us with a slight expletive. I looked round and then realised I had lost Mick. However I soon found him around the corner, shaking slightly and saying he needed a fag! I must admit, as is my habit in some stressful situations, I burst out laughing and tried to console him. Several people clearly resented us. We entered a side gate where a man was reclining in a deck chair. Extending our invitation to him to come to Billy Graham the man got up, and exclaimed rather aggressively "I am not interested, and I'm asking you to leave now!" I don't know if my clerical collar brought the worst out in some people, but on the whole most people were quite polite although not many were interested. Eventually on the night the bus was three quarters full, and to my great delight sixteen people made decisions to follow Christ at Sheffield. The biggest surprise of all came when I found out afterwards that most of them were Church members!

United Marches for Jesus and other Evangelistic Efforts

In addition to the first Billy Graham campaign at Sheffield later there was another campaign by Video Link. This brought Churches together for training to disciple the new converts after the campaign. Prayer was high on the agenda and monthly prayer breakfasts were arranged at this time. There were also "Marches for Jesus" organised and these were headed up by the Pentecostal Church in Jacksdale. Booklets were made available for the participants, and we had to practice the hymns and new songs, most of them composed by Graham Kendrick. We marched along various streets in the Parish, the Pentecostals providing their worship band riding on the back of an open truck, with us all marching behind singing. The number of people converted at this campaign was in no way as many as the Sheffield campaign, but what was important was we were working together as Churches.

I especially enjoyed working with the Pentecostals, and when they began a new Church Plant in the Parish Hall I used to preach there sometimes. I never had a problem, or felt threatened, because another Church was started in my Parish.

In fact I welcomed it with open arms. In addition the Pentecostal Church had a very effective ministry leading assemblies, with their band at the Matthew Holland School.

They also held tent campaigns in the village putting up a marquee near the golf course on Nottingham Road. This attracted quite a lot of youngsters in the evenings, many of which would never go anywhere near a Church.

Evangelistic Visiting and Further Outreach

Some time later I gathered three couples together from the Parish Church to pray and go visiting. A large housing estate was being built near the motorway, where most of the occupants were newcomers to our area. I had carefully drafted a short letter to be handed to each householder. This began with a welcome from the Parish Church, and said that if someone was unwell or had a problem we would be pleased to pray for them. We had never done anything in the Parish like this before, but I felt we should at least try. We were ready to pray on the doorstep, but mainly the idea was if anyone wanted prayer we would go away and pray returning a week later. We had very few people who wanted prayer and we were very discouraged. However as someone has said "If nothing is attempted nothing will be gained."

We also wanted to hire a Working Men's Club for an outreach meeting. The owners were not keen on this but we did find a friendly farmer who allowed us to use the lawn outside his farmhouse. We held two of these open-air events, sitting at some tables with refreshments. These were quite well supported but afterwards this venue was no longer available.

Tower Service and Church Anniversary

The Tower Service is held each year on the Sunday nearest to the seventh of July. This tradition was started way back at the beginning of the twentieth century by the then Incumbent the Rev Charles Harrison. He wanted to celebrate what he called "the first restoration", and the completion of the new South Aisle. The Tower Service is the occasion when the Vicar leads the service from the top of the Tower, some 64 feet up from the ground. This provides a wonderful opportunity to invite different guest preachers to give a Gospel challenge to our community. There is a belief that it never rains on Tower Service Sunday. In fact it only actually rained once in my seventeen years as Incumbent. The year it did we moved into Church for the service.

Each year before the service we processed from the end of Church Lane led by a Salvation Army band, followed by the choir, Guides and Scouts, plus Clergy and Readers all following along to Church. It can be very windy on top of the Tower so one year I actually tied myself to the flagpole. Over the years two of the people I invited to preach declined because they didn't like heights. So facetiously I suggested to one that we could provide him with a parachute and helmet. When he still said no, I asked "Well how are you going to get on when you get to glory?" The service is conducted at two levels, the leaders and preacher on the Tower, with the choir and musicians below in the Churchyard.

Tower Service (1983)
Ray Tew, Peter Thurston (preacher), Ernie Hill & Brian Fox

Each year one or two people gave their personal testimony. One of the most memorable preachers came when I asked CMS for a speaker. The day I watched him come down our drive I suddenly thought I know that face. It turned out to be Peter Thurston whom I had been in the Army with during my National Service. He wasn't a believer then, but had since become a radiant Christian, and then a missionary in India. He had my sons absolutely spellbound as he talked and shared his anecdotes.

Here I feel I must include my thanks to Jimmy Cotterill who always provided the amplifying system for the Tower Service. He also did a lot of electrical and maintenance work for us over the years, saving us hundreds of pounds.

On the evening of the same Sunday we had our Anniversary Service. Originally this had always been a Sunday School event although later we decided to include the whole Church. One outstanding anniversary was when Robert Murray suggested we do a musical called Salty. We also did some Roger Jones' musicals on other occasions. Here I must give a word of thanks to Elizabeth Lester for the immense amount of hard work she put in each year preparing for the anniversary. This, of course, in addition to the weekly choir practices usually on Friday evenings.

Prior to my coming, David and Elizabeth Lester, with Adrian and Maureen Dempster, had joined the congregation. Soon after with their children, nephews and nieces, a regular choir practice was started on Friday evenings. This first began at the Dempster's home. Later when Adrian became Tower Captain practices were held at the Lester's household. After my appointment a senior member of the Church Council wanted to appoint a Choirmaster. This seemed to be a prestige thing to me, so I called a meeting, because I wanted to discover the choir's feelings on the matter, and we finally asked Elizabeth to take the post.

On the Stage

When I first came to the Parish the Incumbent was always expected to sit in his stall during the Anniversary Service behind the children. They were seated on small chairs in front of the chancel steps, on a platform borrowed from one of the local schools. But this sectional platform always left a gap between it and the chancel steps. So as I sat there I became more and more concerned that a child would topple over backwards. Eventually I thought why don't we have our own purpose made platform? One faithful member of the Church was Marjorie Jepson whose husband was a skilled joiner who had made our first new notice board. So I went and chatted with Leon and together we designed and made our own sectional platform. Unfortunately the Church Council was not over enthused about this. So I acquired timber recycled from packing cases given me by a local firm, where Ann was doing a part time secretarial job. We made the top from chipboard and in the end the total cost amounted to £30. Although it was only intended to be temporary it proved to be so useful that we later applied for a faculty to make it permanent. My idea was to cover it with a carpet to match the existing one. Yet this simple decision dragged on for such a long time that some of the new members on the Church Council got utterly fed up. In the end Fred Davidson was asked to advise and arranged this. He had been a member of the Church choir for fifty years and for this had received a medal from the Bishop. Before retirement he had worked as manager for the Co-Op in the furnishings department. Whilst I was away in Chile for a six week sabbatical to my surprise the problem was finally resolved. I still don't know why this simple decision had taken so long to make. On reflection it was, I suppose, just indicative of the indifference of the Church Council to anything new or any form of change.

Drunk on Duty

In July one year, on the same Sunday as the Tower Service, our Deanery organised an open air Communion Service in the grounds of Newstead Abbey. Quite a number of Churches attended and the clergy stood at various points to administer the bread and wine. I can't quite remember why but at the end of the service two or three other clerics decided to hand me their nearly full chalices. My immediate reaction was to ask the lay people who had assisted with the administration to help consume the wine left over. Unfortunately for me however, whether they were high Churchmen or not I don't know, none of them would do so. People expected me to consume it! But I don't drink wine as I have mentioned before, because most protestant Christians in Chile don't. And I have witnessed so many sad cases due to the affects of alcoholism I stand in consolidation with these non-drinking brothers and sisters. However it seemed the people nearby me were leaving me to drink several chalices of the Communion wine. I have to confess that if I had been in my own vestry I would probably have poured it back into the bottle. So there was nothing for it but to consume the stuff! Gulping it down as quickly as I could, because time was of the essence and I needed to get off, I think I consumed most of it. My mother, Ann, Deborah and Elizabeth were all waiting for me. As I began making my way to the car I began to feel dizzy, confirming my worst fears. Getting under way after a little while the road suddenly seemed to be winding all over the place. I was afraid of crashing the car so I pulled over onto the grass verge to wait for a bit. But I still had to get back to lead the Tower Service at 3.00pm. So eventually taking it very slowly we managed to get home safely. Once sitting in our kitchen I explained to the Churchwardens my feeling of inebriation, and inability to attempt to mount the spiral steps to the Tower. Fortunately at this juncture Robert and the Churchwardens decided to ply me with copious cups of black coffee and I somewhat shakily went off to do my duty. I often wonder if anyone one else noticed that day?

Chapter 21
STUDENT PLACEMENTS

Student placements

One of the experiences I most enjoyed, and was such an unexpected blessing, was when St John's College, Bramcote asked me to have students on placement. I think Robin Trew was the first. I remember watching him the first day he arrived, as he came down the drive, with a rather quizzical look on his face. He soon confessed to me that he thought pastoral visiting was a waste of time. As he put it "An endless round of visiting elderly ladies for endless cups of tea does not excite me greatly." However I replied "Well that is part of what we have to do." Despite this we did quite a bit of visiting together, mainly in people's homes, those ill in hospital, and bereaved families.

I learnt from Robin that the college expected him "to reflect theologically" after these visits. I soon began to find that quite helpful and have tended to do that myself since then. Visiting often throws up theological and ethical issues, and gives one a better understanding of basic human psychology. People's comments also raise subjects that people need teaching on, and can be addressed in sermons. With regard to visiting I always made it a habit to pray specifically for the people to be visited. I usually do this before leaving, or just before arriving at their home or the hospital. I feel this is so important, asking the Holy Spirit to give us wisdom and sensitivity. Robin was surprised that many of the people we visited had no previous contact with the Parish Church. He seemed to think that visiting was perhaps a thinly disguised attempt to get them to come to Church, or even get them converted! So he asked me "What are we visiting for?" Robin was to discover that through visiting we were demonstrating a pastoral concern for people, and a deep desire that people would see and understand that God really loved them. Together Robin and I visited parishioners in hospital, in their homes, in old people's homes, those with terminal illness, the bereaved plus funeral planning and follow up visits.

The visits almost always included prayer, sometimes a Bible reading, and occasionally the laying on of hands where this subject had been agreed on a previous visit. Robin was surprised by the ready welcome people gave us, and felt I had a spiritual gift for pastoral visiting as he watched me at work. He said he saw that I had a real concern for people, was at ease with them, able to talk about the Lord and move naturally into prayer.

I never allowed Robin to accompany me just as an observer. I always involved him by asking him to practice what I was doing as we went along, and he gained much confidence in so doing.

He vividly remembered one visit we did. This was to an old lady living in a cottage in the middle of a field. The only access was across a field of cows to reach her door. The elderly lady lived completely on her own suffering with arthritis and deafness. He discovered you had to open the door and go in unannounced, for she would not hear you knock. So we had to risk being impolite, and risk scaring her to death with our sudden appearance, and shout above the high volume of the television.

He said afterwards he could see several reasons for not visiting her. But he came to reflect that we serve a God who is ready to take risks because He loves people whether they own Him or not. At the end of his placement Robin said in his college report "A lot of my apprehension about visiting has evaporated after the actual experience and I am grateful for the opportunity of working with John."

Robin also reflected on a baptism service we held one evening in Hucknall at an Anglican Church having a baptistery. It was an occasion, when because we had several adult candidates, I had asked them beforehand if they would like to be totally immersed. Most were happy with that, except one older lady who understandably said she would prefer sprinkling. The actual baptistery stands near the front with a brick wall surround. Robin commented that I was particularly at home with the service, probably not realising that this was the way I had baptised adults in Chile.

We also used a baptistery in another Church, and this had to be prepared at least 24 hours before to enable them to warm the water.

The important thing I discovered about Robin was that he was really gifted musically and had composed a modern setting to the Communion Service for young people. I had been feeling that our evening service was very formal and needed an injection of something. Consequently I asked him if he would lead a few of the new worship songs that other Churches were beginning to use before the choir processed in. So Robin stood at the front and led some new worship songs, accompanying them on his guitar. After two or three Sunday evenings he came to me looking very disappointed and said "It's not working – people are not joining in - in fact most of them are taking no notice. It seems they feel they have to talk a bit louder to hear themselves talk!" I felt a bit fed up as well, however then Robin said

"What we could try is get the choir to process in and get seated and then sing the new songs." Amazingly this worked and gave us the opportunity to begin to introduce some new worship songs.

He also suggested that members of the Church, who played instruments, could join him. We had recently started a music group to lead the new morning service. Robin found that several members of the choir were also members of the music group. So he suggested to Elizabeth Lester, who led our choir, that she might get music group members and choir to practice the new settings for the ASB Communion Service. Robin was delighted that Elizabeth agreed so the new settings were used for the Easter Day Family Communion. Later members of the music group were also able to boost the congregational singing during the Evening Communion Service as well.

I think one of the most delightful students I had was Humphrey who came from East Africa. As he had no transport another student Beth Palmer brought him in her car. She had previously been lecturer at a teacher training college and was very competent at teaching and preaching. Later she became the Incumbent of St John's, Ilkeston. Humphrey was a very serious student and would sometimes ask members of the congregation if they could help type out his college assignments. He preached very well and usually included a challenge. He had a strong belief in the authority of the Bible and knew the Scriptures well. Preaching from

Annie Jacques, Humphrey,
Beth Palmer & Rev Tony Thistle,
Principal of St John's College

Hosea one day he applied the passage by directly looking at me and saying "What can I do with you John your love is like the morning mist" (Hosea 8 v.4). I shall never forget that! He also believed very strongly in daily Bible reading and prayers with your family.

At one stage Humphrey struggled to eat English food; finding it so different from what he was used to. I think partly due to this he became ill, and so I felt very concerned for him. He was such a long way from his own country, and so missing his wife Rose and their children. So I rang the college and went one afternoon to lay hands on him and pray for healing and some days later he began to get better. I have since found out that he came back to St John's a second time to do a doctorate and later returned home to become head of the Tanzanian Bible Society.

On one occasion Humphrey was looking through our Parish Magazine. Turning over the pages he was suddenly appalled to find so many adverts for Undertakers. "This is not right John!" he exclaimed. "These firms are making money out of bereaved families! In my country the local community makes this their responsibility. They dig the grave, and make all the funeral arrangements. The community also provide all the food for the wake and Church service, and spend a great deal of time caring for the family. Supporting the relatives so they don't have to worry about paying expensive bills at a time of such sadness and distress!" Again another challenge! Surely as Churches and Christians in the U.K. we could do more to support bereaved families in our community, or why not at least provide the refreshments after the service?

Talking to Humphrey one day I confessed I didn't like formal or civic services. In fact a local councillor has asked for a civic service as she lived in our Parish when she was made Mayor. We planned the service together following the lines she suggested. On the afternoon I was very overawed by the "Chain Gang", as she called them, when some six mayors were all seated at the front pew of Church. Consequently I completely forgot I had to meet the new mayor in the porch and accompany her to the front of the Church! So I announced the first hymn and during the singing was highly embarrassed when one of the stewards came to inform me the mayor had not been received and welcomed and was still standing outside! Fortunately we never had any more people made Mayor in the Parish during my time!

All of the students had something to teach me and I enjoyed their friendship and fellowship. The one I especially enjoyed having was Julio Bustos, an ordained Chilean Pastor, whom we had known in Chile when he was still a teenager and had only just become a Christian. One day I had a phone call from Bishop Bill Flagg, Assistant Bishop of Southwell, whom I had previously worked under when he was head of the SAMS. "John, because of your work in South America, and speaking Spanish, I wonder if you would consider taking Julio Bustos on placement?" I replied that I would be absolutely delighted.

So Julio and his wife Tina and two small daughters began coming over on Sunday mornings to our morning service. Tina was a lovely Christian, had grown up in the Pentecostal Church, and was a qualified nurse and midwife. On Wednesdays Julio and I would go visiting together, and he preached several times in Church. Ann and I also used to visit them in their home at Bramcote. We soon became very fond of their two delightful daughters Paula and Natalie. Later Tina gave birth to a small son, so we visited her in hospital and later she asked me to baptise Rodrigo at St Helen's.

Celia Tew, John Jacklin, Tina & Julio with baby Rodrigo

In one of Julio's assignments he compared the English culture in the community to the culture in Church. "Why is this so vastly different?" he asked. "I mean people get so excited and enthused at football matches, but are so passive and obviously lacking in enthusiasm and enjoyment in Church services? And why do people use a whole different vocabulary in Church from down at the pub?" Good questions! Julio had a good grasp of English, and when necessary we were able to discuss things in Spanish. After my retirement Ann and I went to Chile and visited Julio and Tina in the South where they were living and working. He had been asked to head up a new initiative in the city of Valdivia. One warm summer evening we were able to take part in an open-air candle lit Carol Service on Christmas Eve. This was situated in someone's front garden and it was so exciting to witness the beginnings of a new Church.

The last student who worked with me was Norton Taylor, a white South African, who had been a social worker in London for many years. At first he worked with the Pathfinders (the young teenagers) and was good at working with the leaders encouraging them, and praying with them. Although he was also a trained teacher he said he didn't like to work with youngsters. Whilst Norton was with us we decided to use a course called "Saints Alive". We revamped the House Groups under the most experienced leaders and asked Norton to lead one group. He proved he was very experienced in the gifts of the Holy Spirit. He was good at discerning people's spiritual problems and would minister to them in prayer, and the laying on of hands. During the course several people came to discover their spiritual gifts and this helped us to grow as a Church. Norton had decided he would never return to South Africa because of the apartheid. However when things began to get better he felt the Lord calling him to return and became Minister of a very successful Church there.

Chapter 22
PATTERNS OF CHANGE

Changes in Worship

I had promised the Churchwardens I would make no changes for the first year, and I kept my promise, apart from using the new "1980 Alternative Service Book" as all Churches were expected to. The ASB was a momentous thing - the first major change in services since the 1928 "Shorter Prayer Book". Our Church Council discussed the new service book and decided to use it for a trial period. It was to be used twice a month and then we would revise the situation a year later. So after a year we discussed it again and I thought we should give it another year's trial. To my great surprise David Lester proposed the new book be used at all services in the future, except the early morning Communion service. I was even more surprised when the Council agreed to this proposal!

In the beginning the Council at St Mary's, our daughter Church at Westwood, insisted they did not want to use the new ASB. So I invited the Rev Bill Godfrey, from Hucknall, to do a teaching session with St Mary's. Bill had a very gracious manner and even brought his guitar to help us appreciate the new settings to the Gloria and the other sung parts of the Communion service. To my delight St Mary's were won over immediately!

However Ann and I found Church life so utterly different from anything we had ever experienced before. We have been members of the Church of England all our lives, both being baptised as infants. I was perhaps very naive for I was soon to discover that Church music is something people have extremely strong views about. This, of course, applies especially to hymns. I was really surprised to find "Ancient and Modern" (not revised) hymn books still in use, which I accept contain some excellent hymns. Although there was another book called "Hymns of Faith" which was used sometimes. This contained many of the same hymns but the tunes had lower settings, making them easier to sing. Later a very committed older Christian lady called Mrs Smithurst (living in Underwood) asked me to visit her. She very kindly gave me a donation for more copies of the Hymns of Faith.

Eventually people began taking Christianity more seriously. At last the parents of infants were continuing to come to Church after the child's baptism. The attendance at the 10.30am monthly Family Service was increasing each month. We had been using the CPAS (Church Pastoral Aid Society) service, which included baptism. I must confess I preferred the wording, as I had never been able to announce in the old service "This child now being regenerate" with a clear conscience. Ann and I also decided to produce a new service book including many new hymns from "Hymns of Fellowship" and Spring Harvest. It also included hymns from the BBC book "Come and Praise" for schools (which of course the children knew) and some of the "20th Century Hymn Tunes". We decided to call the new book "Worship the Lord" as to be honest we felt that as a Church we were worshipping tradition. Later I will speak more about the new families who began to ask for a regular mid-morning service each Sunday, in addition to the early morning Communion and the evening service.

Changes in the Church Council

From the beginning after a Church Council meeting, as I walked down the Church path, a gaggle of the old guard would be gathered at the gate. They would be deep in conversation until I approached and then the conversation would stop abruptly. I was never privy to these discussions, although it was not too difficult to imagine what they were talking about. Because of the way they had treated Ann I began to loath PCC meetings, and in some ways felt they were a great waste of time. We were meeting every month and almost every time we would regurgitate issues that had been decided at the previous meeting. One reason for this was only half the members came to the meetings, so we had to recap on what had been said at the previous meeting. The other problem was that PCC was getting larger every year; if people didn't get elected at the AGM they would be co-opted. I began praying about this "Lord what's the way forward here?" The answer seemed to be to write to each member. In the letter I suggested that if they were not able to attend the meetings regularly perhaps they should consider coming off. After that the PCC began to get down to a workable size. Some of the older members decided to stand down. Grace suggested it would be good to visit those who had stood down. One of these was Clarice a faithful old lady, who I think was a retired nurse, who had been on the PCC for 33 years, and during my time had never said a word! From then on I would visit her regularly and take Holy Communion to her once a month. I discovered that she really missed the meetings and was in my words "going through withdrawal symptoms!" She enjoyed my visits telling me how she felt about Church matters. I would keep her up to date, and she was extremely supportive.

One day I had to laugh when a local undertaker, the one who had given me so much grief by digging a grave in the pathway, shouted out "Vicar you're doing a great job getting all those people off the Church Council!" I replied I couldn't get anyone off, the members themselves had decided to do that, and of course new people were also getting elected.

Teaching Sessions

Because the first "Teach in" with the Rev Bill Godfrey went so well this gave me an idea that we needed teaching on a number of subjects. So in the future I would invite speakers from outside the Parish to speak on particular subjects. As Adrian has said "If John doesn't know about a subject he always knows someone who does!" During one early session, led by John Prothero from the Bible Society, he asked "What are your plans for the Church?" In other words, how did we see our future as a Parish? I think the Churchwardens were a bit miffed and slightly offended, but to be fair at that time we all found this question a very difficult one to answer. However, John was looking at things from a Biblical perspective. Indeed what we needed was to seek the Lord's guidance, and then John quoted these words "For I know the plans I have for you, declares the Lord, plans to prosper you and not to harm you, plans to give you hope and a future." (Jeremiah 29 v11).

Amongst others we had speakers on the staff of St John's College. From time to time we had missionary speakers, such as Annette Love and Rosemary Brown, (our Link Missionaries in Africa and Bhutan), when they were in the U.K. We also had the Rev Enrique Lago and his wife Margaret spend the weekend in the Parish. Margaret of course is my goddaughter, and I gave her away at her wedding in Chile. Between them they spoke at all our services plus a meeting of the Youth Fellowship.

Ann, Annette Love & Elizabeth   *Ann with Rosemary Brown*

A new thing we decided to do was a Parish Weekend. One year we were very blessed to have Canon Harry Sutton and his wife Olive, who stayed at the Vicarage for the weekend. On the Saturday we were due to use the Church Hall at Ashover, however when we arrived we unfortunately found they had made a double booking so we had to use the Scout hut. Nevertheless on the Sunday Harry preached and we were inspired and encouraged by his gracious style and enthusiasm for the Gospel.

Liz Murray, my Mother, Ann, Elizabeth & David Lester

Fred Crawford & Nora Langton

At least one year we went to a convent in Leicestershire for the day, where the nuns made us so welcome. On Saturday they provided us with lunch and homemade cakes. We also went to Stanton by Dale for the day one year, using the Gateway Centre, the School, and finished Saturday afternoon in the little Church at Dale Abbey.

Another new thing was arranged when Eddie Shirras rang me suggesting we have a "Faith Sharing Weekend". This would in some ways be similar to the student mission, asking Church members to give hospitality to the team for the weekend. Of course this time the members of the team would be all lay members from Christ Church, Harrow. Hospitality was arranged and I especially remember that Eddie and his wife Pamela stayed with Grace Lindley. She was really impressed with her guests and she would often speak of them afterwards. Grace was so pleased to be able to welcome them to her home.

The following year Eddie invited me to bring a team down to Harrow. I have to confess I was a bit apprehensive about this, thinking we could not come up to the standard of his Church. But it proved to be a good confidence building exercise for us. Eddie gave serious sensitive thought to the fact that our Church had no experience in this sort of thing. During the weekend in Harrow members of our congregation gave testimonies during the Christ Church services. Small informal meetings were organised, and Eddie even arranged for our choir to take part in the Harrow Deanery Choir Festival.

Sun Rise Service

During David Grieve's time we agreed to have "Sun Rise" service very early on Easter Day. At first the congregation consisted of just David and myself, and a wonderful old Christian gentleman in his eighties called Mr Palmer. He was a very committed member of the United Reform Church. So at seven in the morning, come rain, wind, sleet or snow we met in the open air at the East end of the Church. Of course one or two people thought we were completely mad. One day Liz Murray said in her wisdom "John why persist in doing this thing in the open air when there is a warm Church building you could use?" So the next year we were happy to come in from the cold and move inside Church. Gradually this new service developed into a United Communion event, where other Churches joined us. Each year I would invite one of their ministers to preach, with David or myself presiding. Before the end of the service the smell of cooked bacon, egg, sausage and tomato wafted over from the North Aisle as we looked forward to consuming breakfast. After that an average of seventy people came and the "Sun Rise Service" was becoming a new tradition.

House Groups

I think it was in my third year we decided to begin House Groups. This again was something new which was becoming successful in many Churches. Perhaps I am giving the impression that all these changes were my idea. Of course that is not the case, as many of these were things I had seen done in Harrow, and things I had to spend time praying a great deal about to see what the Lord wanted. I didn't want to introduce new things just for the sake of change. So after a meeting with the Churchwardens, and others with leadership potential, I appointed House Group leaders to each of the groups. I supplied them with the materials and we would meet from time to time to pray and decide with them subjects for study. I then urged that each member of the group should pay for their booklet, and asked leaders to collect the money. I especially remember that Grace Lindley, the leader of our Mothers' Union, as she was the most industrious and always collected her group's money first. Her group nearly always finished the course material before the others.

From the beginning Grace was so dependable, supportive and faithful. Each Monday morning at 7.30am she would come to pray at the Vicarage with Ann and myself. Grace always remembered our children's birthdays by sending a card. One day she asked me if it would soon be our twenty-fifth wedding anniversary? I wanted to consult with Ann, but as she wasn't there with me I said "Yes, I think it is!" So of course Grace included this in the prayers the following Sunday. Unfortunately I had got it wrong, it was our twenty-fourth. Grace was not at all happy when I told her, but she forgave me. I'm sure we were so different to what the Parish was used to. I recall her saying one Monday morning when she came to pray "Well I think we are beginning to get used to some of your funny little ways!"

Chapter 23
CHURCH GROWTH

Need for an Extra Service

Now some of the new families, coming because of the baptism policy, began putting their views to me. "Why can't we have a regular morning service at 10.30am every week? We find the 9.00am service too early for those of us with children, and we find the evening service is too traditional." I explained the main morning service had stopped before my time when the previous Incumbent finally found the congregation had dwindled to three including himself and the Organist. Eventually I called a meeting of the Churchwardens and House Group leaders. I had listened carefully to the new families, but couldn't possibly provide another service mid morning. Since David my Curate had gone I was now preaching three times some Sundays, especially when going to St Mary's, Westwood at least once a month. I talked with the House Group leaders and explained I had prayed a lot concerning this idea of another service. I therefore believed the answer was in their hands - the lay people. "So it's over to you, each of you has a leadership role in the Church, and I have confidence in you." A phrase often said in those days in many Churches was "It's never been done here before!" Praise the Lord fortunately no one said it that day. Next we then had to discuss and decide the format of the service.

At the time we were already using the ASB book so I said that as Anglicans we needed to use it and adapt the liturgical outline of Morning Prayer. Music was provided with someone playing keyboard usually accompanied by guitars. We used a rota where one person would begin the service using a few biblical verses followed by some worship songs. Another person led the general confession and absolution, or declaration of forgiveness (as I prefer to call it) using "Us" instead of "You".

Next someone followed with a Bible reading taken from the Scripture Union all age teaching material. We then sang a hymn before the children left for their own groups. The smaller children went across to the Vicarage, with Ann and Annie Jacques plus helpers. The Pathfinders staying on the North Aisle with their leader or went to my vestry, which was extremely small and cramped. We said the creed and had some prayers and the adults moved to the Lady Chapel. Instead of a sermon we took part in a discussion on the theme of the day. Or the leader gave a brief talk depending on how confident they felt. After the parents slot we all came back together, the children returned to tell us what they had been doing, and sing a song they had learned. Lastly after a final hymn we all said the grace together.

Adrian said recently that he felt "I was really before my time." I have to say I never really thought of things in that way, I was just concerned to accommodate the new people who had started coming in. During the new morning service I normally sat in the congregation only taking part in leading when it was my turn. However I must now confess that this could confuse people. Sometimes young mums would come in, trundling their baby buggies, wanting to speak to the Vicar about a baptism. They were frequently quite bewildered when they discovered I was actually sitting in the congregation somewhere!

I cannot praise the Lord enough for the success of the new morning service, and we were all so encouraged. This "new thing" was also giving members of the Church a great chance to gain confidence, and develop skills in leadership. A Reader in training said to me last year "The problem with the Church of England is we don't give lay people in our congregations enough chance to take part in leading worship!"

This was something I was really working hard to remedy in my Parish.

One year I asked the Director of Ordinands to preach at the Tower, and thought it would be good to invite him to lunch beforehand. He accepted but said he would also like to come to the morning service as well. I tried hard to dissuade him saying it was very informal, and he could perhaps come to one of the main services at some other time. However to my great consternation he was quite insistent that he wanted to come. Eventually Tower Service Sunday came and the gentleman came into Church for the morning service. I was convinced that I would get a severe ticking off for allowing all these lay people, who were not licensed and had received no formal training, to lead the service. So at the end of the service taking a cup of coffee I tried to hide standing behind the piano. However seeing me he came straight across, and to my great surprise said "John I'm so impressed - I think you're doing a great thing here!"

Training and Lay Involvement

I suppose I should say that I always gave people the maximum encouragement when they were assigned some task. For example when people were doing readings I gave them the passage well in advance. Later we would do a rehearsal, with me sitting at the back of Church to listen and correct anything that needed adjustment. Sitting there I would especially assess their reading for audibility, volume, speed or whatever. Let me give you just one example. One year I asked Don to do a reading during the annual Christmas service of Carols and Lessons. But his reply was "You must be joking John, how could I do that - I'm blind?" Nevertheless he did do it! Stage one was to get him to agree to commit the passage to memory. Once he was ready we went into Church for a rehearsal. Here I asked him to sit on a front pew facing the lectern. We then worked out how many paces it was from his pew to the lectern. Once Don had perfected that I got him to repeat the passage out loud several times. He was quite tall but I can still see him standing at the lectern, slightly bent over in a stooped posture. I was now becoming more and more aware of the enormity of the challenge I had given him. So I said "Please wait, I am coming to pray with you before you read that again." Then placing my hand on his shoulder I prayed for him, asking the Lord to help him to relax, to receive the Lord's peace and enjoy what he was about to do. After going over the passage once more he was then more confident, and when the day came he did a tremendous job. I am sure most of the people, in that packed Church, never realised what a great thing Don had achieved that day!

Recently Maureen said she remembers me saying to her "Don't worry it's the first ten times that are the worst, after that you will begin to become more confident!" Throwing people in at the deep end was sometimes seen to be my speciality! However I always reassured people I was there for them to get them out if necessary! Perhaps I also need to say here that over the years a number of people have said I have the gift of encouragement, and that has been proved to be true - praise the Lord.

Chapter 24
GANG FIGHTS

"It's the Vicar."

For some reason or other one night I happened to look out from our front bedroom window to the Churchyard across the road. Although it was quite dark as I strained to see clearly I could see a small crowd of people standing just inside the wall. So I thought I'd better go over to explore, and putting on my overcoat went to investigate. Standing by our front gate and looking again across the road I could now see twenty-two lads, each one having either an iron bar or chain or some other weapon. It then dawned upon me this was a gang from another village a mile or so away. Suddenly it felt a bit like one of the stories I had read about Gladys Aylward when she was facing a riot in the jail. "You've got to do something" I said to myself. So with my hands firmly in my pockets and eventually summoning up my courage I walked across the road and said "What do you think you're doing, just come out of the Churchyard!" At first nothing happened, but then one of them said quietly "It's the Vicar!" They had obviously not realised who I was! Then as I waited the words "It's the Vicar." were slowly repeated by each lad along the line. Finally I was just amazed because one by one, taking their time, they all climbed over the wall and began walking slowly back down the lane. They had apparently come up looking for a fight with our own village gang. Fortunately this never happened again.

One Friday evening my son Stephen was on his way to choir. Coming out of our gate and turning the corner a teenager came up to him "Are you Ron Brown?" he asked. Stephen replied no he wasn't. "Do you know where he lives?" came the next question. Finally the lad asked Stephen for the time. As he looked down at his watch he was suddenly knocked to the ground, and before he could get up was kicked in the face. Ann and I were at a function in Westward and were suddenly surprised when the police turned up to inform us. Fortunately Stephen wasn't seriously hurt although Ann did take him to the dentist to check that his teeth were all right. Some had been loosened but we were assured that these would put themselves right in due course.

Ron Brown

I would now really like to tell you about the person they were actually looking for. Whilst in the middle of Sunday lunch one day an irate neighbour rang up. "Outside my house is a group of yobs shouting abuse and obscenities at me. If you don't do something I shall ring the Bishop!" Seeing she didn't have the Bishop's number I provided it saying that she wouldn't get hold of him on a Sunday, as he would be out preaching and visiting Churches. The angry lady only lived across the road so I felt I would to go out to discover what the trouble was about. When I appeared she went in, but the lads still stood outside the house. "The lady of the house has complained to me about the bad language and abuse you've given her" I said. It transpired that they had been throwing bits of wood up to knock the blossom off of a double flowering cherry tree in her garden. When the lady came out she was of course extremely angry, and told them off for using a lot of foul language. However what she had not told me was that the lads had only responded by using the same language as she had used!

Some time later I met one of them on his own and chatted with him. I began to realise that Ron came from an extremely difficult and sad home background. His mother had been in a wheelchair for many years and had later died. He had been in and out of care homes over the years. On one occasion he had annoyed a local school teacher who had amongst other things called him a "Thicko". So Ron told me "Right, if people think I am a Thicko I shall behave like a Thicko!" After our first meeting I would often see him as I walked the dog late at night. He was always pleased to talk to me, and one night he crossed the road and said "You know I often used to nick cars, but since I have become a Christian I've changed. Now as I walk down the road and place my hand on a car door the Lord tells me not to do it and He's changed me!" Ron never told me how he had become a Christian, but maybe it happened when the local Pentecostal Church had a tent campaign in the village.

Then one night Peter and Stephen came home late after walking up the lane. "Dad, you know that lad you speak about, well he's had an horrendous accident on a motorbike down near the Horse and Jockey." I quickly put on my coat and went down.

It seemed a friend of Ron's had bought a new motorbike and he had persuaded this friend to let him have a ride. Leaping on Ron had immediately opened up the throttle and had driven at great speed up the hill. It was late, and usually there was little traffic, but this night it was very dark. Unfortunately Ron didn't see an oncoming car and threw himself head first straight into it. Returning home I quickly rang round the local hospitals and discovered he was in the Queen's Medical Centre. Arriving by car I was directed to Coronary Care. It was around midnight but the nurses were all very helpful and allowed me in. As I stood looking at Ron lying there the Night Sister came along to speak to me. "He is very fortunate to be alive!" she told me. "He can't speak to you because he has broken his jaw in six places, and it is all wired up! At the moment we are not sure if his heart has sustained any damage so we are monitoring him." I had just prayed with him when a nurse came with a message. "His father has just telephoned to say he can't get in to see him as he is just off on holiday!" What an incredulous statement - I couldn't believe it! Anyway Ron eventually made a good recovery although I didn't see much of him after that.

Chapter 25
BELLS AND BEETLES

Dedicated Ringers

Bell Ringers celebration at restoration of the Belfry (New Year 1984)

When we arrived in the Parish in 1978 there was already a very dedicated team of bell ringers. Leslie Rawson was then the Tower Captain and he was such a lovely and committed Christian. He had sustained a leg injury down the pit, which made it difficult for him to walk. Despite this without fail he would walk to Church, was there early every Sunday morning, and then had to struggle up all the spiral stairs to the Belfry. Later Adrian Dempster took over as Tower Captain. He was a qualified engineer, very practical at maintaining and looking after the bells, and especially good at training the younger ringers. The first thing that really impressed me was that all the bell ringers actually attended Church services. To be honest this was something extremely exceptional in my experience.

I think it was in 1982 a short time after the Church's quinquennial, or five yearly structural inspection, I made a very scary discovery. We were experiencing some very cold weather and for some reason or other I happened to go up to the bell chamber. Bending down to look at the floor I saw a hole with a diameter of one tenth of an inch. This was quite big and my immediate fear was that this was evidence that we had death watch beetle in the Belfry! I was extremely alarmed because the whole of the Church roof had been replaced in the 1950's because of the damage caused by these terrifying termites that only attack oak timbers. Adrian also found the evidence when he actually fell through the boards, so we notified the Diocese for them to confirm our discovery.

Eventually Adrian took things in hand and decided that the best solution was to replace the bell frame with a steel one. He began to get quotations for the work. Next the bell ringers began the enormous task of removing the sawdust (used for sound proofing) between the floor of the bell ringers' room and the ceiling below. I was soon immensely impressed with the dedicated manner in which the bell ringers - mums, dads, and young people - all began working. Trundling large heavy sacks of sawdust down the spiral staircase taken from under the floor of the bell ringers room. The sawdust then had to be burnt with all the suspected timber down below in the Churchyard. This had to be complied with as ordered by the local authority. Most of the work was done in the evenings after dark, and on more than one occasion complaints came from niggling neighbours about the smoke. Once this was completed the bells had to be lowered and I remember one Saturday sitting with my feet dangling through the hatch, easing through the largest bell that became a bit jammed. All the bells were finally lowered safely to remain on the floor under the Tower for nearly a year.

Adrian continued to oversee the work and saw the new steel bell frame installed. Two new bells were also ordered one was paid by Leslie Rawson's brother Gerard in memory of their father (who had been Churchwarden), and one in memory of Vera Wood. This made up the full compliment to eight, and the new frame was made to accommodate them. Taylors, the famous firm of bell founders in Loughborough, wanted to know why we had not asked them to provide and hang the bells. I had to reply that this was because our bell ringers had done so much work themselves, and had saved us between three or four thousand pounds. About a year later the bells were re-hung and soon in action again. My good friend Rev Tom Curtis, with whom I had worked in Chile, came up from Gloucestershire to preach and re-dedicate them.

Later at the time of the Selston Carnival it seemed good to enter a float to express our thanks to people for their support to get the bells up and ringing again. So taking some pews from the North Aisle we mounted these on a lorry kindly made available by Richard Wright. It was suggested that for the float choir members and the Vicar should robe and sit on the pews. Passing along Portland Road I distinctly heard at least two parishioners say "Oh looks like the Vicar up there - but I'm sure it's only someone dressed up like him!"

Chapter 26
BUILDING A TEAM

A Team Ministry

After the Ridley Mission Robert began to grow as a Christian, and was going from strength to strength. First he began by serving as Churchwarden. But soon we had an increasing number of young teenagers so Robert and Liz took on the task of leading the Youth Fellowship. If I remember correctly Keith and Jill Dring had been doing that at first. Robert often felt the young people knew their Bibles better than he did, but he was available to serve the Lord, depending on Him, and was developing new skills. The group had several Bible reading marathons in Church. Later it was suggested that they might like to go to a Christian Family Conference. Robert and Liz, with their two small children, Ann and myself all went down to Wadebridge. Robert hired a mini-bus, and the idea was that we should share the driving. However because I was absolutely exhausted I slept most of the way and Robert did all the driving. It was a great week, even though we had a terrible storm one night damaging our tents, and leaving most of them lying flat in the morning.

Cyfa Bible Marathon (July 1985)
Deborah Jacklin, Robert Murray,
Sarah Hoskins

One day Robert and I went to a service in St Alkmund's, Derby. It was a renewal meeting and a call was made for leaders to go forward for prayer. We were sitting together so I suggested we both go forward, but Robert insisted that only applied to me, as I was the Vicar. However we went forward together, and whilst I was there I distinctly heard one of the team use the words "kneel down and worship" in Spanish. The lady was of course speaking in tongues, so I asked her if she knew what she had said. She replied she had no idea, as she was new on the team, and her companion was the theological student.

I had been praying for Robert and believed the Lord wanted him to become a Reader. So later I asked Robert to think and pray about Readership, saying I would not ask him for his decision until a year's time. He agreed and to my great delight was selected and eventually licensed in 1992.

Robert was also responsible for several new initiatives including the men's group called "Mash" or Men at St Helen's." Celia had received much help during the "Saints Alive" course, and felt the Lord was also calling her to go forward for Readership. She was selected and then licensed at the same time as Robert. Earlier I had appreciated David Lester's work as treasurer, Churchwarden and Vice Chair of the Church Council. David had been good at guiding us through some of our difficult discussions so I asked him to consider Readership, and he was accepted and licensed. Later I recommended Brian Fox for Readership at St Mary's, Westwood, for I had witnessed how good he was at working with young people. In addition Dorothy Carter became licensed as a Reader at St Mary's. At some stage I put forward Brian for ordination and he was accepted for training. But he was disappointed as this was only as a Non-Stipendiary Minister, so he decided to join the Pentecostal Church and has since been Pastor of his own Church.

Celia Tew, Robert Murray, John Jacklin, Dorothy Carter & David Lester at Dorothy's licensing as a Reader (1994)

Norman and Iris Ramsden, with Fred and Norma Crawford, also did some very dedicated work with Pathfinders after David

Pathfinders led by Norman & Iris Ramsden (1987)

Grieve left. Norman knew his Bible well and had already studied full time at Bible College. I used to ask him to preach sometimes even before becoming a Reader. I remember him saying that he wasn't too keen to tog up in cassock and scarf, so I assured him that I wouldn't expect him to do that too often. Later I recommended Norman for ordination and he was accepted, but he eventually decided to move away and join another Church. Quite recently Brian Fox said to me "You know John I have never met anyone who had recommended so many lay people for leadership roles as you have!"

Leadership Style

On reflection I think my team approach, so different to many clergy at that time, was due to my background. Also to be honest I could never have done all that the Rev Victor Hubert Simons, my predecessor had done. He had cleared the Churchyard of an enormous jumble of broken headstones, forming a wilderness into a rose garden, and spending hours every week regularly cutting the grass. That is of course in addition to, as I have been told, staying up late at night doing the Church accounts. All of which I feel must have contributed to his premature death, and sadly not being able to enjoy his retirement. We owe him an enormous amount of gratitude for such a faithful ministry.

After I left technical school in my first job I served an apprenticeship as a carpenter and joiner with the Greater London Council. There I always worked with a majority of older men who were prepared to encourage and help me. After National Service in the Army for two years I worked as a draughtsman, and finally as surveyor in the architects' offices of the Greater London Council. There were always architects and surveyors ready to answer my questions and lend me technical books. Finally working as a missionary in South America, working in the prison and hospital, I developed a very strong conviction of what has been called the priesthood of all believers. I learnt so much from both Pentecostal and Anglican lay people there.

We see in the New Testament that all Christians are servants of God, "A holy priesthood" and "A chosen people, a royal priesthood, a holy nation etc." (I Peter 2 vv4 and 9). The New Testament knows nothing of a priestly caste. Paul writing to the Corinthian Church says that any member could speak in the services if they had something to contribute (I Corinthians 14 vv26-29). He also spends considerable time teaching about the body of Christ, and the gifts Jesus gives to every member "for the common good" (I Corinthians 12 and Ephesians 4vv11, 12 etc.) I love to hear people coming to the front to speak of an answer to prayer, or some encouragement or challenge the Lord's given them. Many clergy seem to feel threatened if people in the Church disagree with them, or come up with different ideas to their own. Surely it's all about leadership and discussing and talking things through, and most of all praying with others about everything to discover what the Lord's plans are. I must affirm that it was usually only after prayer over a period of time that I would ask a person to take on some task or office. I had to be sure this was what the Lord wanted. In nearly every case this worked out. I had been ordained and commissioned to build the Kingdom, and was under the Lord's authority. I never felt threatened, but was humbly confident the Lord knew what He was doing. I remember when I was Curate in Harrow someone once asked Eddie Shirras (my Vicar) "Are you in charge here?" To which Eddie replied "No lady I'm just the manager!"

The Williamson Family

In 1985 a few days before we were going on summer holiday I received a letter from New Zealand. Paul was a clergyman in the South Island where he had five Churches over a scattered area. He was coming to Nottingham to study for a Masters degree at St John's College, Bramcote. Could I offer him a

Paul & Dale Williamson (1985 – 88)

job as a part time Curate? I replied briefly and quickly saying that I needed a Curate who would be responsible for the daughter Church, St. Mary's, Westwood and that I would look into it when we came back from holiday. It was such a wonderful surprise, as I now had no Curate, but honestly I could not see the Diocese agreeing to it. On return from holiday I contacted the Diocesan office to be told there was no chance of a part time curacy full stop. What I didn't realise was Paul had already written to them and been refused! I wish I could remember all the details now. However incredibly to my amazement and disbelief the Diocese, within a few weeks, changed their mind. The Lord was obviously in charge of the situation. For suddenly they promised to pay him a half stipend, if the Parish could provide a furnished house! The Parish soon came up trumps assembling all sorts of stuff, including kitchen utensils saucepans, bedding and furniture. My wife Ann gave them a couple of bunk beds with mattresses, and I made them a bookcase.

Prior to that we received several letters from them and in one Dale was asking about the riots in Jacksdale? This made me smile, but I tried hard to reassure her that there had never been any. In another letter I discovered from Paul that when you buy a house in New Zealand this not only includes carpets and curtains. It must also include kitchen equipment, such as cooker, fridge, and washing machine etc. So the whole exercise was something of a challenge and learning curve for us as a Parish. Paul was very practical and later bought an old Peugeot, big enough for the family, and did quite a bit of mechanical work on it. He was a great asset because he had been involved in the renewal movement in New Zealand. So when we decided to use the "Saints Alive" course I asked him to train the group leaders. At times he found it difficult to balance pressure between Parish duties and studies for his degree. Yet he made time to do some re-ordering of St Mary's, sealing off the Choir area to make an extra room, and extending the worship area with a small platform and Communion rail. We were sad when the Williamson family returned to New Zealand and very soon I began to feel the pressure of being on my own once again.

When I first came to the Parish I had a full time Curate, called Jim Robinson, based at St Mary's, Westwood. He was eventually made Priest in charge of Shireoaks some time after David Grieve left. Now after the first few years we were experiencing growth in numbers, but with no other professional staff I struggled, so I spoke to the Archdeacon saying I just couldn't cope and would have to leave the Parish.

Later during a training day at Mapperley he said "John I have a proposal for you to consider. Because of the Sheffield Report we are not allowed any more clergy, but I wonder how you would feel about considering having a Church Army Officer?" After a few days I rang the Archdeacon to agree with the idea of going ahead with his proposal. Eventually Paul Knight was appointed as Lay Pastor at St Mary's. In his job description I stipulated that he could do everything a clergyman could do except the sacraments, the Rev Ernie Hill would do these. This seemed to work reasonably well. Paul was very practical and amongst other things he was responsible for the new kitchen and toilet extension at St Mary's. After about three years Paul asked if I would recommend him for ordination and he was accepted for training and later became Incumbent of his own Parish.

Chapter 27
MONEY MATTERS

Money Matters

In the beginning the Church Council was reluctant to spend any money, so everything had to be done on a shoestring, especially for things like the platform. If money was needed I was told to ask the Patron or speak to a local land owner. Then much later in the early nineties I received a letter from the Archdeacon saying all Churches had to have a Stewardship campaign. I ignored this but within a few months I received a second letter. Eventually I took the issue to the Church Council, and said that I didn't agree with the idea. The Council listened carefully as I explained it would involve going round the Parish knocking on doors and asking people to give money. In addition we would have to have a dinner where people were expected to sign pledges, and furthermore we would have to pay a Stewardship Organiser some £2,500 from the money raised. I found the whole idea quite unacceptable, so the Council asked me if I had an alternative idea. At the back of my mind I remembered someone once said "The Lord's money is in the pockets of the Lord's people."

So I explained that I felt strongly that what we needed was some teaching on Christian Giving. I was delighted, and somewhat fearful, when they responded with something like "Well John do what you feel is best!"

I had been thinking about Church funding for some time and after further prayer contacted John Finney (later Bishop of Pontefract) and our Diocesan Adviser on Evangelism. Sitting in my study after a brief discussion I explained I had tried to find a course on Christian Giving without success. John didn't know of one, and said "Compile one yourself John, you've had plenty of experience over the years!" What a challenge! So after contacting the CPAS (again with little success) I began to go through my Bible. One little book I got hold of was by R.T. Kendal, (that's still in print), called "The Gift of Giving". At the beginning of our course I began by telling of how Ann and I had been tithing since before we were married, and how the Lord had always provided for us so generously.

The first session began by looking at the story of Abram, in Genesis chapter 14, where the patriarch rescued his family after they had been taken prisoner.

This episode came many years before the Jewish Law was given, and speaks of Melchizedek, who is a type of Christ in the Old Testament. And "Abram gave him a tenth of everything" (Genesis 14 v 20.) In fact tithing was the custom of the ancient people in Abram's time, so this was nothing to do with the Law for that would come many years later.

Please also read Hebrews 7 verse 11 and the following verses speaking about Jesus. The course included five sessions to be used by the house groups, with Sunday sermons based on the weekly themes. Incredibly at the end of the course I think our Church Giving went up by at least 23%! Norma Crawford was treasurer at the time and I had asked her to do a graph of our giving. She was doing a great job, but very hesitant to do this. However what we discovered was that 70% of our members were only giving £1 a week!

Later I was summoned to appear before the Diocesan Finance Committee, and give account of what we had done. Standing before the Board, consisting of several Canons, they were soon offended when I told them that the Stewardship Advisers were unnecessary and should be made redundant. The money they were being paid was needed by the Churches! At the end I was asked to leave copies of our Giving Course. Finally I was told by one Canon I had annoyed the Board, and should not have made my opening remarks. I listened with benign indifference and went straight home.

Fred Crawford & Norma with Celia Tew

Chapter 28
FAMILY ROOM EXTENSION

The Facilities at St Helen's

As I mentioned earlier, the refreshments after my induction were provided in the Parish Hall, which was at least half a mile away, and some people became lost getting there. Later numbers at our services began increasing, with new families of parents with children coming in, but we still had no proper facilities, not even a decent toilet and nowhere to serve tea or coffee, or a kitchen. Nora Langton said I was the first person use the term "Church Family". This was in no way meant to be exclusive, but on the contrary as I began to listen we could now hear different regional accents from different parts of the country. The wonderful thing was that everyone was now becoming accepted as part of the Lord's family, especially the new families coming in - so different from the beginning when Rev John Finney (later Bishop of Pontefract) tongue in cheek said to me "The trouble with this Church is, that it wants people to come, but they must be nice people just like us!"

The Church had a Scout Troop attached but we had no facilities suitable for meetings – they were in fact meeting at the Methodist Church. At the side of our Vicarage was a small site and the Scouts were keen to erect a temporary hut there. I personally went to look at this sectional building but found some of the sections were already rotten, so this was not really the answer. The Bishop also advised me against this idea. The only toilet for the Church was situated in the corner of the Churchyard and was very basic, with very damp crumbling stone work, and was frequently vandalised with the windows smashed, and the light fuses often removed. After much thought and prayer I approached our Church Council about a Church extension. The idea of having a separate hall across the road from the Church also raised a serious problem. Church Lane could be very busy at times not only with cars but also with people on motorbikes. As we found, when we held Sunday School in the Vicarage, it could be quite dangerous for children and the elderly to cross the road. We needed something adjacent to the Church. In fact my predecessor had thought of enlarging the clergy vestry, which was extremely small. Eventually it was agreed that an architect be asked to carry out a feasibility study. Dare I say the Church Council was very concerned to know how much? Then fortunately to their great surprise an anonymous benefactor came up with cash - actually Ann took a part time job in order to pay for it! I think this has always been kept completely secret until now!

When I was a Curate at Christ Church, Harrow the Church hall was some half a mile away. Under Eddie it was soon felt that there was a need for some facilities nearer the Church. There was a very limited amount of land to the east end, and this was on a hill. However Kenneth White, a very experienced architect was engaged to design an extension adjacent to the Church. (He had written two small books published by Grove Books; "Shrines for the Saints" and "Centre for the Servants".) Christ Church, Roxeth, had been designed by the acclaimed Victorian architect Sir George Gilbert Scott, so I suppose it was no surprise that when Ken White submitted his first design, Harrow Council rejected it out of hand. However he was not to be beaten and the second scheme was not only approved, but they later gave him an award for design! Because Ken White was obviously such an experienced and successful architect our Church Council gave me permission to invite him to do a feasibility study. He had two practices one in London and one in York, and I really admired him as a committed Christian and Churchwarden. He personally completed a feasibility study, and showed us one or two possible designs. Then tragically within a short time he died of a heart attack, so we were back to square one. I was personally very saddened and disappointed at Ken's death.

Later we approached John Severn, who had a practice in Nottingham. He came with considerable experience of working with historic Churches. His first design was to be thrown out by our District Council, and although he went to appeal at the Home Office he was unsuccessful. Over the next months we wasted much time as a partner of Mr Severn submitted different schemes to the District Council. We appointed Adrian Dempster as Chair of our building committee. I remember we arranged a meeting with two of the planning officers in Church, so they would have some idea of how behind the times we were without any proper facilities. During the meeting I was absolutely flabbergasted when one said "Oh when I was in Sunday School if we needed the loo we just went behind the trees at the back of Church!" I was highly annoyed and said "We are getting new families coming to Church now, plus some elderly ladies in their seventies and eighties, we need some proper facilities!"

Much later Adrian and I met some other planning officers at their offices. Taking our new architect Mark Stewart, we had been discussing things for an hour and were getting nowhere. Then to our amazement one of the planners looked at Mark and said "Well what sort of a building would you like to put up?" Adrian later said he was astonished at the sudden change

110

in the tenor of the meeting. But I knew that the reason was I had asked at least five other Churches to be praying for the meeting.

However I retired in 1995 and there was little sign of the new extension then. I have thought several times that I would probably never see the "Family Room Extension" as we at first called it, built in my time. But now praise the Lord, because of Adrian's perseverance, vision, determination and faith, and the superb support and encouragement of Fiona, the present Incumbent, the new extension is complete and its facilities widely appreciated by everyone. The whole idea had started around thirty years ago, and maybe I had forgotten Jesus words "With God all things are possible." (Matthew 19 v26.) Recently reading a book written in the 1930's on the spiritual life, the author quoted one of the early Church Fathers as saying "He that is in a hurry hinders the work of God." Something I am trying to learn in my old age!

St Helen's Church Family (1995)

Glory to God
"Gloria a Dios"
By John Jacklin

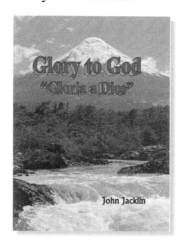

John and Ann Jacklin worked with the South American Mission Society in Chile from 1962-1975. They served first in the south among the Mapuches and then in Santiago. John has a wonderfully self-deprecating air about him, whether it be for his supposed inadequacy with Spanish or pastoral work or evangelism or whatever. The reality is - and this is his point - that it was God who used both him and Ann to do mighty, and often extraordinary, things in Chile. The recounting of those deeds makes a great story, reminds us what a great God we have and also what great missionaries God has raised up.

Told by his doctor not to go to South America because of his father's imminent demise, John found the will and strength to obey God's call and God responded by giving his father 22 more years to live, years which included visits to the Jacklins and their growing family.

Humour and poignancy mark the book, not least in the sections dealing with the Pinochet coup and its aftermath. It was during this latter time that God's power and grace were particularly evident in some of the people the Jacklins encountered.

Read it and give God the glory. And add a word of thanks to God for giving John the courage to write it.

Robert Lunt